HENRY PARK'S
ROAD TO A
MILLION
WORKBOOK & JOURNAL

"The best investment is in yourself"
- Henry Park

HENRY PARK'S

ROAD TO A
MILLION

HENRY PARK

EDITED BY ROBERT MILLER

ISBN 978-0-9975887-8-1

Pineapple Upside Down Cake

This book is like a **pineapple upside down cake** because I am going to begin with the end and end with the beginning. **Henry Park's Road to a Million** is not about making gazillions in the stock market like Forrest Gump did when he invested in Apple Computer (AAPL) — or about how Gordon Gekko made a killing by trading on insider information with BlueStar Airlines. As we say on Wall Street, I am going to tell you "how the hog eats the cabbage" — the unabashed truth about creating and protecting great wealth — whether you want to hear it or not.

But before we begin let's take a painful but realistic look at the world around us. We have been to hell and almost back this last year. Our world has been turned upside down like a pineapple upside down cake. But at least there are some cherries on the top. As this book goes to print America and most of the world is emerging strong and ready to kick ass and take names.

Finally, we must develop the ability to be ahead of the curve — to predict trends and changes and react quickly to leverage them to our advantage. Like the immortal words Walter Gretzky passed on to his son Wayne: "Skate to where the puck is going, not to where it has been."

So where is the puck going in global business? Let's take a look at the future of business because we're never going back (and that's a good thing).

The pandemic has accelerated the digitalization of business almost beyond our wildest imaginations. And it has given government, business, and media more control over our lives than any of us ever thought possible. The pandemic was like a **Trojan Horse** that snuck in at night.

I could do your homework for you but then you would never learn. I encourage you to commit to making a major ongoing investment in yourself by doing some research and developing your own theories and opinions about the future of business. Then, and only then, will you be able to create your own personal investment strategy.

To get you started here are some of the trends that I am watching:

- How products and services will be delivered (Postmates, Instacart, Drizly, Grubhub, drones) — look for more disrupters like Amazon Prime, Uber).
- How we will shop, pay, and bank (Stripe, cryptocurrencies, CoinBase, Nubank, Shopify).
- How we will work (virtual workplaces, Zoom, business tech, Clubhouse).
- How we will travel, socialize, and play (Roblox, virtual communities, online gambling, entertainment, TikTok, OnlyFans, SpaceX, Peolton, NextDoor).
- How, where, and what we will be eating (plant-based foods, super-foods).

- Wellness (biotech, Headspace, medical cannabis, med tech, telemedicine, virtual fitness training, genetics).
- Environment (climate change, green energy, NextEra).
- Financial Services (fintech).
- Alternative Energy (EVs, solar, wind).
- Return to Globalization (Mercado Libre).
- Investing (Robinhood, CoinDesk).
- The Graying of America.

Hopefully, the sun is shining where you are and you're alive (if you're reading this) but we are far from out of the woods. It's all about perspective — the glass half empty or the glass half full. The Dow is screaming toward 40K, and residential real estate is on fire. Expect some speedbumps (aka "corrections") on your **Road to a Million.** But remember that the world of investments has changed forever. You can't just invest "Warren Buffet" style by walking into See's Candies® and seeing, touching, feeling, and tasting your investment. And forget your grandfather's approach of "buy good companies and hold them forever" (Pan Am, TWA, Sears). Welcome to a "Brave New World of Investing" — it's time to jump onto my investing party bus. See you onboard. Party! Party! Party!

So where is the puck going in global business? (Draw a diagram.)

Welcome to the Layer Cake

You're born,
you take shit
get out in the world
you take more shit
climb a little higher
take less shit
till one day you're in the glorified atmosphere
and you've forgotten what shit even looks like.
Welcome to the layer cake, son.

— J.J. Connolly
Layer Cake (2000)

enry Park's Road to a Million is about one thing — it's about teaching you how to make enough money so you don't have to take shit off anyone. It's about getting you to the point where "you've forgotten what shit even looks like." There are three parts to **Henry Park's Road to a Million.** There are my **Books**, there's my **Facebook Group,** and there are my weekly **Zoom Classes** — all with the same name.

Live with no excuses,
travel with no regrets.

What is the most important thing in your life?

My family is the most important thing in my life —my amazing wife Andrea — and our five wonderful children — Katie, Preston, Dylan, Audrey, and Dominic.

To My Father,
Jung Sil Park

If you're born poor it's not your mistake, but if you die poor it's your mistake.

— Bill Gates

Your only limit is your soul. What
I say is true — anyone can cook…
but only the fearless
can be great.

— Chef Gusteau
Ratatouille (2007)

READ THIS FIRST!

READ THIS FIRST!

I know I'm probably going to get a lot of shit about it, but this book is written **raw and unplugged** — you are going to get the real **Henry Park** — no filters and no attempts to be PC. I know a lot of people who act like they are someone who they real not or someone they want other people to think they are. For example, I feel that some (not all) people on Facebook (especially in my industries of loans and real estate) hit "like," add comments, and generally act very friendly for the purposes of recruiting and having people join their company, but then with someone that they don't think they are going to get business from (for example their competitors) or someone they hate on, they are not all nicey nicey.

Making money is not a value loss proposition — if I make money doesn't mean you're going to make less. The world is big enough for everyone — let's all be millionaires!

WHY THIS BOOK MATTERS

Reading is essential for those who want to rise above the ordinary.

— Jim Rohn

Getting RICH, unless you win the lottery or inherit a fortune from a rich uncle, is a process — not an event. And reading this book should be a process — not an event.

Like life, what you get out of *Henry Park's Road to a Million* pretty much depends on what you put into the experience. So, I am going to make some suggestions on how you can get the maximum **ROI** from my book.

You can choose to take my suggestions seriously or you can laugh them off. Like any investment, you need to decide how much you want to invest and what you expect in return. If you invest your time and energy wisely you can become a millionaire.

I believe in learning things once and using them forever. The tools, tactics, strategies, and philosophies which I share with you within these pages are the net product of thousands of deals over my lifetime. Many of the deals were phenomenally successful — and some of them were

WHY THIS BOOK MATTERS

horrible failures. But, at the end of the day, every one of them was a priceless learning experience. I hope to save you some blood, sweat, and tears (and money) by providing you with this toolkit for becoming a millionaire — or even a billionaire.

Everything in this book relates to my own life in some way. I have used these tools, tactics, strategies, and philosophies to succeed in business and investing. This book matters because you can use my toolkit to prepare yourself for your own journey. Toss my toolkit into your trunk and add more tools along the way.

The first time you read this book skip through it selectively to get familiar with its contents. There is an introduction — **Dare to Be Rich** — and a summary — **Rest Area**. And there are twelve chapters in between. After skipping through once invest some quality time to study all the chapters one by one.

If you are anxious and just want to fast-forward to the bottom line you can skip to the **Owner's Manual** in the back of this book where you'll find a **7 Step Action Plan**.

Keep in mind this is your book — take ownership of it. Turn down the corners of pages. Highlight text. Make notes in the margins. And, most importantly, take advantage of the blank sections that I have provided for you to plan your **Road to a Million**. This is an *interactive* book — it's all about **YOU**. You have a Journal at the end.

I am not trying to recruit you, convert you, or convince you of anything. My goal is to simply inform you, educate you, empower you and inspire you to take control of your finances and make the most money you can with the least possible effort as quickly as possible while making an enormous positive impact on your life and the lives of your family and community. If that sounds like a mouthful it is. But what's life if you don't reach for the stars — all of them — each and every day of your life. Hold on tight and get ready to jump onboard my private party bus about to take off on **Henry Park's Road to a Million.** Don't bother to put on a seat belt — I've got you.

Life's not about having a lot of money; it's about having a lot of options.

— Chris Rock

HI. IT'S ME HENRY!

```
PRIVATE
ROAD
NO
OUTLET
```

I don't regret my past, I just regret the time I
Just regret the time I've wasted on the wrong people.

— Wiz Khalifa

I wrote this book because of a few reasons. One, I was tired of people talking shit on all rich people. Not all rich people are evil, but I thought maybe it's because most people don't know how to make money. So, I am going to teach you all the tricks I've learned from my buddies that worked on Wall Street and take it to Main Street. Now for full disclosure, I'm not licensed as a stockbroker or anything like that and I am not asking you for money. In fact, if you follow me, you may lose money. I am merely showing you that it is possible for you to become a millionaire.

HI. IT'S ME HENRY!

Some of the best relationships begin with a simple introduction. Hi! I'm Henry Park and I hope that this book — in some way — will change the way that you look at **wealth**.

This book is being published shortly after my forty-seventh birthday and during the second year of the pandemic that turned the world upside down.

Henry Park's Road to a Million is my fourth book. Last year I co-authored three books with Robert Miller (the editor of this one). This book is intentionally much different than my other books because it's only purpose is to get you on your own **Road to a Million**. If you're already a millionaire maybe it will help you replace the "M" with a "B".

This book is not about me — it's all about YOU! What do I mean by that? Although I am going to share a little about my **Road to a Million** in **Part Two — My Backpages** — you are not me and your road will be entirely different. Why do I say that? Because no two roads to a million are identical because no two people are identical. And that's the secret of wealth — each of us has to plan and follow our own road to a million and have the courage and determination to reach our own final destination.

Great wealth often comes from great poverty. That's what happened to me. But that doesn't necessarily mean that you have to be poor to become rich. One of my favorite quotes comes from food critic Anton Ego in Disney's 2007 computer-animated comedy film *Ratatouille*: **"Not everyone can become a great artist, but a great artist can**

HI. IT'S ME HENRY!

come from anywhere." I believe that not everyone can become a millionaire, but a millionaire can come from anywhere.

This book is written raw and unplugged in sixth grade English and as simply as possible to present some pretty complex and highly sophisticated investment concepts. It is not a textbook nor is it offered as a motivational book. It has one — and only one — purpose. And that purpose is to inform and inspire you so that you are able to look at money and wealth in a completely different way than you might have ever imagined.

If I can change your perspective on what a millionaire is and show you how you can become one, I will have achieved my objective in authoring this book.

A few months after the pandemic began last year, I formed a group on **Facebook** — *Henry Park's Road to a Million.* **My Facebook Group** quickly grew to over 1,500 members who joined to learn about investing. I host a weekly **Zoom Meeting** at 5:00 PM (Pacific Time) every Friday and invite you to join my Facebook Group and participate in my weekly classes. Information about my group and classes is at the back of this book and my classes are available on my **YouTube Channel.**

I look forward to meeting you online and maybe in person someday. Perhaps our paths have already crossed. The world is small and is becoming smaller every day.

Make this book and your **Road to a Million** a game-changing experience. You have the power to create and

HI. IT'S ME HENRY!

protect great personal wealth and live the lifestyle of your dreams.

Before you get too deep into this book, I encourage you to visit **HenryParkNow.com** and learn about who I am and what I do. Maybe you will be able follow me better.

I am not a coach, mentor, or guru. I am mortgage banker and a self-made multi-millionaire who is passionate about investing and creating wealth so my family and I can live a lifestyle that others dream of. When you learn a little more about me you will discover that my lifestyle is not about Gulfstreams and Ferraris — it's not about luxury.

My lifestyle is about travel and personal and family growth. And, finally, it's 100% about my wife, Andrea, and our five children. The reason that I make money is to provide safety and unique experiences to Andrea, Katie, Preston, Dylan, Audrey, and Dominic.

I wish you the best on your **Road to a Million**. Please drop me a line and let me know how you're doing: **Henry@HenryParkNow.com**.

Henry Park
Las Vegas

1/3 of Americans believe
that they
will one day become
millionaires.

Now that I've got your undivided intention, I'm
Gonna say this and run under condition one
Promise me you gon' stack, promise me you gon' ball
Promise me you'll invest three fourths of it all
For what? So your kids, kids, kids can have some
    cheese
Can't get with it? Get, get, get, get, get on your knees
'Cause wealth is the word
Rich is round the corner from the curb
Don't like what I like? Shoot me a bird

              — *Hollywood Divorce* (2016)
                OutKast

HENRY PARK'S

ROAD TO A
MILLION

WORKBOOK & JOURNAL

I bought a dozen volumes on banking and investment securities and they stood on my shelf in red and gold like new money from the mint, promising to unfold the shining secrets that only Midas and Morgan and Maecenas knew.

— *The Great Gatsby* (1925)
F. Scott Fitzgerald

Right now,
before
you read
the next page,
join my
Facebook Group
Henry Park's
Road to a Million

ACCOUNTING

TRADE # 58 SELL 7 SHARES OF EXPI
(PRICE OF $140.71)
TRADE # 59 SELL 100 SHARES OF TELL
(PRICE OF $3.87)
TRADE # 60 BUY 20 SHARES OF BMBL
(PRICE OF $15.94)
TRADE #61 BUY 200 SHARES OF GTBP
(PRICE OF $5.68)
TRADE #62 SELL (TO CLOSE) 1 APR PUT CONTRACT
@ STRIKE OF 93 FOR GME
(PRICE OF $52.62)
TRADE #63 SELL 50 SHARES OF SQQQ
(PRICE OF $16.53)
TRADE #64 BUY 500 SHARES OF HTZGQ
(PRICE OF 0.94 CENTS)
TRADE #65 SELL 500 SHARES OF HTZGQ
(PRICE OF $1.96)
TRADE #66 SELL 200 SHARES OF GTBP
(PRICE OF $7.04)

CURRENT CASH BALANCE $4,106.80
EQUITY: $4,106.80

HENRY PARK'S ROAD TO A MILLION

Henry Park
April 5 at 2:31 PM ·

If your in the group you will be happy to know that I started at $1,000 and as of now 10 months later I'm up over $4,000. $4,106.80 to be exact. 😄 400% Return on investment (ROI) isn't bad considering most hedge funds only return 20% on average. We still have one trade left which is BMBL. Can't win them all. I'm still holding on that for now. So let's be patient. I'm going to go hunting for the next good trade. ✌️

Hope lies in dreams,
in imagination
and in the courage
of those who dare
to make dreams
into reality.

— Jonas Salk

DARE TO BE
RICH

FREEWAY
ENTRANCE

1

I knew that if I failed I wouldn't regret that, but I knew the one think I might regret is not trying.

— Jeff Bezos

DARE TO BE
RICH

You can't always get what you want
You can't always get what you want
You can't always get what you want
But if you try sometimes, well, you might
    find
You get what you need

— You Can't Always Get What You Want
The Rolling Stones (1969)

**Don't EVER believe that you can't get what you want.
If you want '…ten chocolate chip cookies. Medium chips. None too
close to the outside.' Then have the balls to get your 'ten chocolate
chip cookies with medium chips and none too close to the outside'.**

3

This 25th day of April, 1498, being invited to dine by his Holiness Alexander VI, and fearing that not content with making me pay for my hat, he may desire to become my heir, and reserves for me the fate of Cardinals Caprara and Bentivoglio, who were poisoned I declare to my nephew, Guido Spada, my sole heir, that I have buried in a place he knows and has visited with me , that is, in the caves of the small island of Monte Cristo all I possessed of ingots, gold, money, jewels, diamonds, gems, that I alone know of the existence of this treasure, which may amount to nearly two millions of Roman crowns, and which he will find on raising the twentieth rock from the small creek to the easy in a right line. Two openings have been made in these caves, the treasure is in the furthest angle in the second, which treasure I bequeath and leave to him as my sole heir.

The **Count of Monte Cristo** is a story that you might know from French author Alexander Dumas published in 1844 — or maybe from the several adventure films. It's about a French sailor, Edmund Dantes, who was wrongfully, but deliberately, accused of treason at age 19 and sent to prison. He spent 14 years in prison before escaping.

In prison, Dantes met a man who told him about a hidden treasure on the Island of Monte Cristo — and he crafted a brilliant strategy for those who betrayed him. One day Edmund Dantes escaped and went to Monte Cristo and found the treasure of gold and jewels worth $9 billion (in today's dollars) which had been buried for 350 years. Dantes transformed himself into "The Count of Monte Cristo" and the rest is history.

How many stories of buried treasures did you hear about growing up? Like me, did you dream about finding a buried treasure one day? Well, you just found one. I am going to share my personal treasure chest and give you some priceless treasures that will help you **Dare to Be Rich.** Keep **Henry's Treasure Chest** in the trunk of your vehicles on your **Road to a Million.** Stop at rest areas along the way, pop open your trunk, and look through the treasure chest for some roadside assistance to get you to your final destination — **RICH.**

There are **7 Secret Treasures** that I am sharing, and they are all that you will need to keep you on the road in the right direction and at the proper speed to guarantee you a safe, fun, exciting, and prosperous trip from where you are now to where you're going.

1

Know Why You Want to Be Rich

Regardless of WHAT we do in our lives, our WHY —
our driving purpose, cause, or belief — never changes.

> — Simon Sinek
> *Start with Why:*
> *How Great Leaders Inspire*
> *Everyone to Take Action*

Why do you want to be rich — why are you reading *Henry Park's Road to a Million*? Until you can answer this question from your heart and from the bottom of your soul you may never really be rich. And before you can even begin to answer the question you must decide what the word "rich" means to you. **Rich** is a relative word that entirely depends on your personal perspective. **STOP** right now and think about **WHY** you want to be rich and record your thoughts on the next page.

KNOW WHY YOU WANT TO BE RICH

Instructions: Describe **WHY you want to be RICH**. Your WHY may change several times during your lifetime — maybe even several times before you finish reading this book.

2

Be Badass

Just keep moving forward and don't give a shit about what anybody thinks. Do what you have to do, for you.

— Johnny Depp

The definition of **"Badass"** is highly subjective so I am going to tell you what it means to me. For me Badass means someone who has a well-defined "why," has a laser focus, and continues to move forward like the Energizer Bunny against all odds or like Arnold as *The Terminator*.

Urbandictionary.com has this to say about **BADASS: Ultracool motherfucker. — Dirty Harry**.

You don't have to wear a leather jacket and have a teardrop tattoo to be badass — just be sure you're not a poser wearing a fake Rolex and driving a C Class with an AMG emblem that you bought on Amazon.com for $11.19.

BE BADASS

Describe why you think you're **BADASS**.

9

3

Put the Pedal to the Metal

Straight roads are for fast cars, turns are for fast drivers.

— Colin McRae

Velocity is very important on your **Road to a Million.** It's important that you jump on the road and put your pedal to the metal immediately after you complete all of the chapters of this book.

Pack up your stuff, set your navigation, put your toolkit in the trunk and hit the road. Don't pass GO and don't collect $200. Keep on truckin' until you hit the $1 million mark.

Remember that it's not just how fast you get from here to there — it's all about following your trip plan, reading your map, keeping your eyes on the road, negotiating turns, avoiding hazards, and minimizing roadkill.

PEEL OUT

<u>Instructions:</u> Let's get started, right now, planning your own trip on your **Road to a Million**. Why are you going? When are you planning to leave — when do you want to get there? Who's going along with you (if anyone)? How are you going to get there? What's it going to cost (in time and money)?

4

Don't Look Back

Don't look back unless it's a good view.

— Tupac Shakur

Only fools look back — don't be a fool! Before you leave on your **Road to a Million** rip out your rearview mirror and tear off both side mirrors. In fact, get rid of all the mirrors in your life because you're going to learn not to give a fuck about what happened ten years ago — or ten seconds ago.

Remember in *Forrest Gump* when Forrest's platoon was ambushed, and he kept going back and forth from the ambush site to the LZ (Landing Zone) to rescue his buddies? Forrest might have been a dumb son of a bitch, but he was a hero because he was focused on saving his buddies. He was under fire but kept going — never looking back.

DON'T LOOK BACK

Instructions: Fuggeddaboudit! That's right — forget about everything in your life right now unless it's something that makes you happy or motivates you. Don't look back on the Monsters in your life that keep trying to fuck with your mind — don't allow them to be roadblocks on your **Road to a Million**.

5

SPEED LIMIT 70

Follow the Rules

It's hard to drive at the limit, but it's harder to know where the limits are.

— Sterling Moss
British Formula One Driver

I would like to say that the only rules are that there are no rules. But we both know that there will always be rules. One of the laws of successful investing is to know which rules you need to follow, and which rules you can risk avoiding.

First of all, investing is highly regulated so to avoid sharing a cell with Bernie Madoff or Gordon Gekko you need to know and follow all of the legal rules. That being said, regarding everything else you can be like Gordon Ramsey (*Hell's Kitchen*) and make up your own rules. The only exception to that one is that you need to follow my rules!

FOLLOW THE RULES

<u>Instructions:</u> Right about now you might be saying: "Rules, to god-damned hell with rules! We have no rules. In fact, we don't need rules. I don't have to follow any stinkin' rules, you god-damned cabron and ching' tu madre!" (Adapted from "Badges" in *The Treasure of Sierra Madre* (1927). Anyway, list your rules here and come back to this page and list mine.

6

Don't Go EMO

I don't want to be at the mercy of my emotions. I want to use them, to enjoy them, and to dominate them.

— Oscar Wilde
The Picture of Dorian Gray

Emotions are the wildcard of investing. You need to have none — but you need to understand everyone else's emotions. Emotions drive markets — pure and simple. Easier said than done! What you need is a virtual frontal lobotomy. Before scientists in the mid-1950's created antipsychotic and antidepressant medications to deal with mental illnesses the frontal lobotomy was a cruel procedure that left patients dull and without emotions. That's what happened in the 1962 novel by Ken Kesey and 1975 film *One Flew Over the Cuckoo's Nest* starring Jack Nicholson.

Instructions: Let's get started, right now, planning your own trip on your **Road to a Million**. Why are you going? When are you planning to leave — when do you want to get there? Who's going along with you (if anyone)? How are you going to get there? What's it going to cost?

7

Take Risks

The biggest risk is not taking any risk.

— Mark Zuckerberg
Co-Founder of Facebook

Risk is the mother's milk of investing. Without risk there would be no investing because there would be no volatility and there would be no opportunity to speculate.

The secret to **risk** is understanding it and knowing how to manage it. Like greed — risk can be good or bad. It all depends on which side of the equation you position yourself.

If you are not willing to consistently take risks and "face up" to the consequences *every time,* then you should toss this book in the trash and play a video game on your iPhone. Your **Road to a Million** will be full of risks.

TAKE RISKS

Instructions: Life, and especially investing, is full of risks. In fact, risk is what life's really about. Record, very openly and honestly, how you FEEL about risk — and how much risk you're willing to take on your **ROAD TO A MILLION**.

Now it's time for some motivational stuff. But keep in mind that it's not about me and my **Road to a Million** — it's all about you.

In **Chapter Two — My Back Pages** — you are going to learn about me and what motivated me to become a millionaire. You see all of us have our own reasons for wanting to be rich. I was born in Guam (a U.S. Territory) where my parents met and then we moved to Hawaii before landing in California. By the time I was 5 I had already lived in 3 places.

My parents were born on Korea and my PC label is "Korean-American" because I was born in part of America — U.S. Territory of Guam.

Anyway, we eventually settled in Hawaiian Gardens near the Los Angeles/Orange County border. The 2000 U.S. Census reported that 63% of the city's population at that time was "Hispanic or Latino of any race." When I was growing up there it seemed like almost everyone was Latino. Because we must have all looked the same to them, the Latinos classified me as a "chinito." But the problem was that they thought that all "chinitos" were rich.

MOTIVATION

My family was not rich. You'll learn more about that in a little while. But, for now, take my word that we were not rich. When the homeboys discovered that my parents were Korean, they immediately thought about the Koreans that owned liquor stores and I was permanently labeled as a "Crazy Rich Asian," Well, "two out of three ain't bad,"

Remember that I told you to stop looking back? That's easier said than done. When I was about 12 years old, I rode my bike down the San Gabriel River Bed (which is alongside the 605 Freeway) from Hawaiian Gardens to Huntington Beach. I did that as much as possible to escape the barrio to see how the "rich people" lived.

So one beautiful summer afternoon I arrived at the beach and cruised around looking at houses — **California Dreamin'**. I saw an open house sign, parked my bike, and walked into the house to look around. When I reached for a flyer the real estate agent grabbed it away from me, so I asked, "how much is this house?" He looked down at me with a **very racist white privileged expression** on my face and barked: "Much more than you'll ever be able to afford kid." "Woke" wasn't in then.

I believe that extreme wealth often comes from extreme poverty and evidentially Jordan Belfort agrees with me (see below). You shouldn't have to watch movies like *Wall Street*, *The Wolf of Wall Street*, *Boiler Room*, *Trading Places*, *Glengarry Glen Ross*, *Barbarians at the Gate*, *Liar's Poker* — or even *Scarface* or *Blow* to motivate you to get started right now on your **Road to a Million**. The best way to become a millionaire is to learn how to think like one.

21

THE WOLF OF WALL STREET

See those little black boxes? They are called telephones. I'm gonna let you in on a little secret about these telephones. They're not gonna dial themselves! Okay? Without you, they're just worthless hunks of plastic. Like a loaded M16 without a trained Marine to pull the trigger. And in the case of the telephone, it's up to each and every one of you, my highly trained Strattonites, my killers. My killers who will not take no for an answer! My fucking warriors who'll not hang up the phone, until their client either buys or fucking dies!

Let me tell you something. There is no nobility in poverty. I've been a rich man, and I've been poor man. And I choose rich every fucking time. Cause, at least as a rich man, when I have to face my problems, I show up in the back of a limo wearing a $2000 suit ...and $40,000 gold fuckin' watch!
Now, if anyone here thinks I'm superficial or materialistic. Go get a job at fucking McDonald's, because that's where you fucking belong! But, before you depart this room full of winners, I want you to take a good look around at the person next to you, go on. Because sometime in the not-so-distant future, you're pullin' up to a red light in your beat-up old fucking Pinto, and that person's gonna pull up right alongside you in a brand new Porsche, with their beautiful wife by his side, whose got big voluptuous tits. And who will you be next to? Some disgusting wilder beast with three days of razor-stubble in a sleeveless moo-moo, crammed in next to you with a carload full of groceries from the fucking Price Club! That's who you're gonna be sitting next to.

So, you listen to me and you listen well. Are you behind, on your credit card bills? Good. Pick up the phone and start dialing. Is your landlord ready to evict you? Good. Pick up the phone and start dialing. Does your girlfriend think you're a fucking loser? Good. Pick up the phone and start dialing! I want you to deal with your problems, by becoming rich! All you have to do today ...is pick up that phone and speak the words that I have taught you. And I'll make you richer than the most powerful CEO of the United States of fucking America. I want you to go out there, and I want you to RAM Steve Madden stock down your clients' throats. Till they fucking choke on it till they choke on it and buy 100,000 shares! That's what I want you to do. You'll be ferocious! You'll be relentless! You'll be telephone fucking terrorists! Now, let's knock this Motherfucker out of the park!

— Jordan Belfort (Leonardo DiCaprio)
The Wolf of Wall Street (2013)

ONE

He had one of those rare smiles with a quality of eternal reassurance in it, that you may come across four of five times in life. It faced, or seemed to face, the whole external world for an instant and then concentrated on you with an irresistible prejudice in your favor. It understood you as far as you wanted to be understood, believed in as far as you would like to believe in yourself.

— F. Scott Fitzgerald
The Great Gatsby (1925)

ONE
HENRY PARK
NOW

To see the world, things dangerous to come to, to see behind walls, draw closer, to find each other, and to feel. That is the purpose of life.

— Walter Mitty (Ben Stiller)
The Secret Life of Walter Mitty (2013)

Don't be a poser, kiss ass, or wannabee. You can never be a 'used-to-be' because life is like a roller-coaster — continuous ups and downs. You can be bankrupt and a millionaire ten years later — and (hopefully not) a millionaire now and bankrupt in ten years. So don't be a poser, kiss ass, or wannabee — be yourself. Don't smoke cigars or snort coke because you think it's what ballers do. If you live your life through the lives of others you will soon realize that you have no life at all.

Welcome to my world — **The World of Henry Park.** By the time you finish this book or maybe even this chapter — **Henry Park Now** — you will have discovered that Henry Park is that the real Henry Park and the Henry Park not that you might have believed Henry Park to be. That's a lot of **Henry Parks** — and I'm talking about myself in third person but it's my book and I can do that if I want.

I am an **Investor, Entrepreneur,** and **Advisor** *and* a self-appointed **World Lifestyle Ambassador** (which I will explain in a little while).

I love my **Wife and Children, Dealmaking, World Travel, Food, Music,** and **Friends** (pretty much in that exact order). You notice that my list does not include money or things.

My happiness comes from my passions — **My Family —** **Doing Deals** — and *Experiencing* **the Faces and Places of the World.** I believe that life pretty much gives you what you give it and I give life as much of Henry Park (there I go again third-party) as I can. My editor describes me as a **Raconteur** (Google it) because I share amusing stories about my experiences — like those in this book.

The Invitation Didn't Mention That It Was a Black-Tie Event

H enry Park is a pretty simple guy — at least I think so. Remember **WYSIWYG** (what you see is what you get)? That's me! I believe that I'm the poster child for "the millionaire next door" — or maybe the kid on the milk carton who went missing and ended up in Neverland with Peter Pan and the Lost Boys.

I admit it. I suffer from the **Peter Pan Syndrome** — men who never grow up (and never want to). My theme song is Bob Dylan's *My Back Pages* (1964) — "Ah, but I was so much older them, I'm younger than that now."

I prefer my 1997 Toyota Supra over my Porsche 911. I prefer cooking a gourmet meal at home over a pretentious "used-to-be the place where the elite went to eat" steakhouse. I prefer hanging out with my family over hanging out with my "bruhs" at Pelican Hill or Shady Canyon. And I prefer flying commercial over owning my own private jet (I invest the difference — which is huge even though I travel almost constantly). Don't get me wrong. I enjoy partying with my homies, It's cool to fly on private jets as long as someone else is paying for it.

World Lifestyle Ambassador

Zoo animals are ambassadors for their cousins in the wild.

— Jack Hanna

What's a **Lifestyle Ambassador**? What do you want it to be? For me it means that I life my life my way (just like Frank Sinatra) and openly share my lifestyle with the world.

I am not a guru, life coach, or mentor. I do not feel qualified to advise others how to live their lives. But I do feel qualified to share with others how I live my own life with purpose and passion. And I believe that I know enough about making money that there is great value in sharing my knowledge and experience in business, finance, and investing.

Lifestyle Ambassador — I love the way it sounds. But that does not mean that my branded lifestyle is for everyone. In fact, just because it works for me doesn't mean that it will work for you — or does it?

29

INVESTOR, ENTREPRENEUR & ADVISOR

To get rich you have to be making money while you're asleep.

— David Bailey

I couldn't have said it better myself but let's say it again: "To get rich you have to be making money while you sleep." You need **multiple streams of income**. That's why I am an **Investor**, **Entrepreneur**, and **Advisor**.

I have been an **investor** ever since I had more money than I needed to pay my bills. I invest aggressively in all types of **stocks** — and also actively in **real estate.**

I'm a serial **entrepreneur** — I currently own 20 companies and am on top of every one of them — they are all profitable.

My day jobs are **Mortgage Banker, Bond Trader,** and **Financial Advisor** — but I don't really think of any of them as jobs because I love doing deals. And I wouldn't trade places with anyone anywhere. My biggest challenge I have each day is deciding who I want to be.

REAL ESTATE INVESTOR

Ninety percent of all millionaires become so through owning real estate.

— Andrew Carnegie

I believe in **real estate investing**. It is a great feeling to own something you can touch and see — something you can walk on and into. Real estate investing is much different than investing in stocks for that reason.

Like investing in stocks, I invest in real estate for both short term and long term. Short term real estate investing is like trading stocks. I look for properties that I can buy at a low price and sell at a higher price within a relatively short period of time (Fix and Flip) — or properties that I can buy at a low price and keep in my real estate portfolio for monthly income and long-term appreciation (Fix and Rent).

Build a **real estate portfolio** on **Your Road to a Million** for income, appreciation, safety, and diversification. Like stocks, value is critical and so is **location, location, location**.

The world keeps getting smaller and smaller and I keep getting more excited about **global real estate investing**. The Latin American market is *super caliente* now and getting hotter every day. If you are interested in real estate investing in the U.S., Latin America, or any part of the world, let me know. It should be a fundamental part of your investment portfolio

31

WORLD TRAVELER

You need not even listen, just wait… the world will offer itself freely to you, unmasking itself.

— Franz Kafka

Well I don't know about unmasking during this global pandemic but I agree with Kafka on the rest of it. I never traveled much until after my father died in 2015. My world turned upside then and, when I woke back up, part of my metamorphosis was to start traveling.

Always studious and trying to learn Japanese so I could read the sushi menu, I was the "married-with-5 children" version of Anthony Bourdain. I was traveling and eating like a crazy. And with travel came self-discovery. I will never be a monk but the more I discover the world — the more I discover myself.

Over the past six years I have visited 28 countries — some of them several times. With almost 200 universally recognized countries in the world I have some more to go.

WORLD TRAVELER

Some of the places I have been:

Bahamas	Thailand
Mexico	India
Dubai	Belgium
Abu Dhabi	Iceland
Japan	Netherlands
Taiwan	England
Hong Kong	Singapore
Macau	China
Argentina	Korea
Peru	Panama
Australia	France
New Zealand	Egypt
Vietnam	Turkey
Cambodia	Belize

GLOBAL FOODIE

Once you decide on your occupation… you must immerse yourself in your work. You have to fall in love with your work. Never complain about your job. You must dedicate your life to mastering your skill. That's the secret of success… and is the key to being regarded honorably.

— Jiro Ono
Jiro Dreams of Sushi (2012)

I love sushi and so when Netflix started streaming *Jiro Dreams of Sushi* in the summer of 2012, I dreamed of going to Tokyo for the best sushi in the world. The film was a documentary about Jiro Ono, an 85-year-old sushi master. You've got to watch the movie because you'll learn a lot about life.

Determined to eat the best sushi in the world I kept calling Tokyo for reservations at the little 10-seat sushi-only restaurant. I kept calling and calling and was unsuccessful — which was unacceptable to me. So, I decided to call the concierge for my American Express Black Card.

The American Express Concierge told me that I *might* be able to get a reservation by booking 3 nights at the Peninsula Hotel — so that's exactly what I did. Bottom line? I spent $7,000 for me and Andrea to have $350 sushi dinners. And it was worth every dollar.

Eating with Takashi Ono

I met Jiro Ono's second son Takashi. When you watch the movie, you'll learn that there's a tradition in Japan that the oldest son is expected to take over the father's business. Since Takashi Ono was the *second* son, he started his own sushi-only restaurant called Sukiyabashi Jiro Roppongi. Chef Takashi was trained by his father at the original Sukiyabashi Jiro in Ginza and appears in the documentary sharing his experiences and relationship with his world-famous father — the legendary Chef Jiro.

Jiro Dreams of Sushi will teach you a lot about dreams and passion — about perfection and excellence — about business and life. I often wonder what would have happened to me as my father's first son if I would have followed in his footsteps. Would my destiny have been to become a gas station tycoon?

Jiro Dreams of Sushi

DJ Dosa

I didn't come up as a DJ, so I don't play by DJ rules.

— Deadmau5

Music has always been a passion for me and probably keeps me from going crazy in my day jobs. My thing is **EDM** — Electronic Dance Music — aka "dance music," "club music," or sometimes even just "dance."

EDM is played at clubs, raves, and festivals and includes a broad range of percussive electronic music played by DJs like me.

As DJ Dosa I ignore what's trendy and play the music I love. A lot of work goes into DJing — more than people could ever imagine. I always wanted to be a DJ so I could share my love for music with other people. The most important thing for me is to quickly develop and continue to build a magical relationship with the people listening to my music. For me, that's what DJing is all about.

Check out DJ Dosa on
#Sound Cloud

http://soundcloud.com/henry-park-511304407

Who's the **Real Henry Park** and **Where's Henry Now?** First, like Jay Gatsby in *The Great Gatsby* (F. Scott Fitzgerald — 1925), there's a lot of shit out there about me. People wonder how a poor Korean kid from the hood could become a self-made multimillionaire. I know people talk shit about me — because it gets back to me all of the time. And I really don't give a fuck — I don't care what those losers and haters say about me. Seriously! You know Benedict Cumberbatch — British actor dude? Listen to what he has to say about that: "If you have an over-preoccupation with perception and trying to **please** people's expectations, then you can go **mad**." I don't want to go mad — no fucking way! So, fuck the motherfucking haters! There, I said it. And that's all I have to say about that!

Now for the second question. **Where's Henry Now?** Most of the time you can find the answer to that question on **Facebook** or **Instagram.** I could be at home (and that includes several locations), or I could be with Andrea and our five kids at Spring Break in Maui or taking Andrea to Paris (France —not Perris, California), or in Tokyo trying sushi from a **World Class Itamae.**

Where's Henry NOW?

Can you find me in the above photo and identify the location? (Hint: white shirts and pants and red bandanas — no masks).

TWO

P R O L O G U E

Great geniuses have the shortest biographies.

— Ralph Waldo Emerson

I am not a great genius by any means and this book is not my biography but it's important that you know some things about my personal history to understand how I think about money and my investment style.

We all have our own stories — that's what makes the faces, words, thoughts, and dreams of the world's billions of people different from one another. My father had his story and — although it has had the biggest single impact on my life — my story is almost the opposite of his.

My father believed in the American Dream (and so do I) but thought that by working hard every day that someday he would be able to retire and enjoy his life and family. That day never came because his life was cut short by cancer. Now I am going to share how that woke me up and forced me to slow down.

TWO
MY BACK PAGES

Every secret of a writer's soul, every experience of his life, every quality of his mind, is written large in his works.

— Virginia Woolf

Invest a couple of hours in yourself and write down your own BACK PAGES. What has happened during your lifetime to make you who you are. What do you need to forget and what will motivate you on your Road to a Million?

To tell you how I started on my **Road to a Million** is to go back to the beginning. Growing up I had a father who was always working. Coming from Korea he struggled trying to learn a new language and prove for his family. My dad started as a gardener and joined the military so he could come to the United States. My mom was a travel agent working for Korea Airlines. They met in Guam and that was where I was born. Shortly after I was born, they moved to Hawaii since my dad's side of the family had moved there. That's where my brother was born. After that we moved to Los Angeles.

Growing up we always struggled financially. My mom became a waitress at a Japanese restaurant. My father ended up working for my aunt and uncle as a cashier at a Shell gas station. Back then minimum wage was $3.25 an hour so that's what my dad made. It was at that point that there was a turning point in my life. All the Shell dealers were required to remain open 24 hours a day 7 days a week (including holidays).

Since my dad so desperately needed the hours, he would work at the gas station 7 days a week. At night, since it was always slow, my dad had a little makeshift bed where he would try to catch some sleep in between customers. So, my nightmare began — that was the last I saw of him for a few years. I remember hating life because I wanted to see my dad — I even hated the gas station for taking my dad away from me!

My dad somehow had me convinced that he was working for the family — I believed him. You see we were so fucking poor, living It in a 1-bedroom apartment in

Hawaiian Gardens. It was a HUD low-income apartment. Don't get me wrong — some of my best childhood memories happened in that apartment. But when you come from nothing all you want is the best because you have nothing.

Well anyways my dad eventually went to night school to become a mechanic. He went to Cypress College and became an ASC Certified Mechanic. I loved those years — we would go fishing and camping on the weekends and play basketball all the time. I loved it!

But then one day my father had an opportunity to buy a Shell gas station of his own. He knew someone who was selling his gas station. By this time, my aunt (who was rich in my eyes) owned 3 gas stations and my dad looked up to her. My dad sat us all down one day and told us that he was borrowing money to buy the gas station. We were excited but didn't know what that meant. He said we all needed to help out. I was down for the cause. Our whole family was. And so, from the age of 12 my brother and I would work as cashiers after school and on weekends at the gas station.

I didn't mind at first. But then my dad came up with a crazy plan. My dad had borrowed a lot of money to buy the gas station. And it came to a hefty interest payment each month. My dad wanted to pay the loan off quickly so here is the crazy plan. You see 99% of the "garages" are closed on Sundays. So, my dad's genius plan was to open Sunday so he could capture all that business. From a business perspective it was great! My father convinced us that someday we would be able to afford to live in a house — maybe even one with a pool.

47

The Gas Station

In my opinion that was one of the worst decisions ever! It seemed like the only time I could spend with my father was working together at the gas station. I hated that gas station with a passion. My dad did eventually buy a small house a few years later and by the time I was 18 years old he bought the house of "our dreams" (pool included) in Cypress. I kind of felt it was "his" dream because by the time he bought the house it was time for me to go to college.

So, you see for me I didn't want to make the same mistakes my father did. **I was going to make money fast and quick and a lot of it. I eventually made a lot of money. Millions in fact, But I was going to do it right.**

I knew I wanted to have kids, but I wanted to have the house and everything, so they didn't suffer while I was making money. I wanted to spend time with them and play with them and do the things my dad did with me when he was a mechanic before he got the crazy idea to borrow money and buy the gas station.

In our "glory days" we went camping and fishing and I thought the only way to do this was marrying someone much younger. My wife Andrea is 7 ½ years younger than me and I love her more than the whole world. We got married. We both sacrificed. Saved money. Andrea drove a Daewoo and I drove my 1997 Toyota Supra (which I still have and drive). We never spent money. Always saved. We didn't have kids for almost 10 years after we got married. And then, right when we were planning on starting our family (with millions of dollars in the bank) the crisis of 2007 hit. And what seemed like overnight we lost all our hard-earned money.

We went from living in Huntington Beach 2 blocks from the beach (remember what happened to me when I was a kid at the open house in Huntington Beach?) to shopping for groceries at the 99 Cent Store. It was really that bad!

You see all our savings went nowhere. We tried to save our mortgage company. We had never taken a vacation. We had never slowed down enough to enjoy anything. I felt devastated and Andrea felt the same. So, we decided we weren't going to wait anymore. And so, in 2008, our daughter Katie was born, and our family began to grow (now we have 5 kids). Before I realized it, I got sucked into working crazy and long hours. You see the mortgage business is like real estate — it's a commission business. And all that would have continued until I got a call one day from my mom.

My mom called me that summer of 2014. I was at a Secondary Marketing Conference in San Francisco. All I remember was that I was in the middle of a meeting with some other bankers and my phone kept ringing and ringing. I finally excused myself and answered the phone. I asked my mom, "mom, what's going on?" I had just seen my dad and Andrea and our kids just a few days before.

All I remember was that my mom was saying that my dad had Stage 4 Pancreatic Cancer. I was like "WTF"? I didn't even know where the pancreas was in the body. How could this happen? You see up to this point I never knew anyone who had cancer before. All my uncles and aunts were alive. I mean I heard of people getting cancer but not anyone I knew or cared about. It was always some neighbor's mom's cousin. So, you could see how shocked I was. I remember my hand trembling as I Googled "life expectancy stage 4 pancreatic cancer". It said, "2 months"! I just about lost it! I kept crying uncontrollably. You see I was going to redo everything with my father. I had to show him his son was successful! I had money and was going to be a good father — a better father! But little did I know that I was following right in his footsteps. Don't get me wrong. I used to think my dad was horrible in business. You see my father owned a gas station in Norwalk and his customers were primarily older white people and Latinos. And every single time my dad would fix someone's car he would tell them to buy a Toyota. Dad said that Toyota made the best cars and that they last forever without costing a lot for repairs. I remember that when I was younger, I would ask my dad, "but if you all your customers buy Toyotas you won't get any business!" I just remember him beating the crap out of me that day and telling me that I needed to learn to "be a good person." I didn't understand then — but I do now. My dad was the most honest man I have ever known.

But I remember not having a lot of money twisted my soul. I mean when it came to making money, I was good at it. Maybe too good. I wanted to be like Gordon Gekko from the movie *Wall Street* growing up not knowing who I became was not who my dad was proud of.

Anyways so finding out my dad was going to die I was in a panic mode to relive my life. Kind of like the movie *Bucket List* I needed to right every wrong. But I learned the hard way unfortunately that life was not "rewind" button in my life — nor in anybody's life. There are no "do overs."

Whatever time is lost is lost. You can only fix the present and the future. My dad had a kind soul. He meant well.

But he realized in the end that there's no "redo." Kind of like in the movie *Click* where Adam Sandler realizes there's no redo. And who was I to rub it in my father's face? Anyways the cancer grew quickly and soon... the inevitable happened.

The next two months I spent every day with my dad. Word of advice — when a loved one is in hospice care the best thing you can do is to make them comfortable. I don't know what I was thinking, and I was so stupid now that I reflect back — I wanted closure. I wanted to know all the things I already knew my dad to be. He loved me. He really did. He made mistakes but it was almost like he wanted to beat the answer out of him. I should have been more courageous, but I was the little boy again in my eyes. In the end I did get the apology I wanted which was like a knife in my heart. My dad told me, in his dying days, "Just be a good person and spend time with your kids and love them. I always loved you. I wanted the best for you and your brother. Coming from Korea back then — a very poor country — I didn't want you to suffer. So, I worked hard for our family. And somehow I got you to hate me and for that I am truly sorry." It just killed me when he said that. I knew he loved me. I knew.

So, there is the pain in my heart. I'm so guilt-ridden. After my dad died, I went back to working. I tried to somehow reshape my past but realized the past is over. I kept thinking of what my dad told me, "I don't care how much money you have, just be a good person." I kept asking myself, "What was he talking about?" My kids go to private school. They live in Newport Beach. "What does he mean?" I was sad, confused, and hurting big time! My life was a pineapple upside down cake.

And then one day I came home late as usual, and the kids were already asleep. I turned on the TV and there was the show *Keeping Up with the Kardashians.* And I just kept thinking and thinking, "Why the hell am I coming home so late? What happened to me putting the kids to bed like I had promised myself?" Since I was a little boy, I wanted to have a family and dreamed of playing with my kids and putting them to sleep at night. So, I asked myself, over and over again, "Why the hell am I more concerned in what the Kardashians are doing in their lives when I have my own life to live?" So that was how the concept of *KeepingUpwiththeParks.com* was born.

At that moment I decided to take massive action — I was going to become a different person, I decided to become the person my dad was telling me about on his death bed. My dad left me a gift. I couldn't change the past, but I can change the future. So now I have become reborn. Not the same person. I am going to be the best husband to Andrea — and the best father to our 5 kiddos. Thank you, Dad. I get it! I love you with all my heart.

This book — my fourth — is dedicated to my father, Jung Sil Park. He will remain in my heart and mind forever.

I have openly shared **My Back Pages** with you to help you understand that although this book is titled **Henry Park's Road to a Million** it's not about money. Life is all about love and the people we love. Let's begin! Day 1

E P I L O G U E

All death reminds us that nothing is promised, only that life was worth it.

— Shannon Alder
300 Questions to Ask Your Parents
Before It's Too Late (2011)

Everything in this book — every letter, every word — every photo, every graphic — every quote, every lyric has a purpose. It may seem like a patchwork quilt, but it was designed and written and shared to inform you and inspire you to live the life as you want it to be lived.

I would gladly give millions of dollars to go back in time and have a conversation with my father about his life. I would listen to his stories about how he grew up and how he dreamed of coming to America with his family. I would ask about his dreams of owning a house and a business. Looking back at my father's life he was the American Dream — a poor immigrant who left his country for a better life for his family. He will always be my hero. I love you Dad.

Hawaiian Gardens

Happy Days and Wonder Years

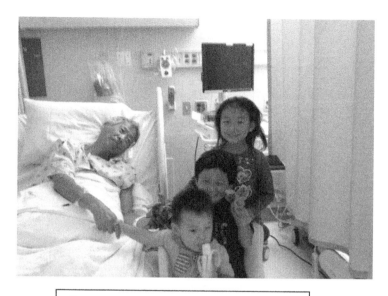

Dad Holding on to Life (Literally)

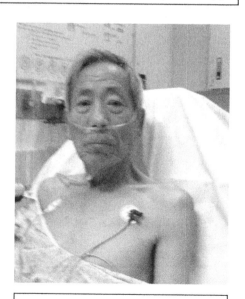

What was Dad thinking?

Remembering Grandpa

They told you **wealth** is about having more **money** than **anyone else**.

They **lied**.

Wealth is about having **more freedom and time than anyone else**.

Happy Days & Wonder Years Again!

In my younger and more vulnerable years my father gave me some advice that I've been turning in over my mind ever since. 'Whenever you feel like criticizing anyone,' he told me, 'just remember that all the people in this world haven't had the advantages that you've had.'

— Nick Caraway
The Great Gatsby (1925)
F. Scott Fitzgerald

THREE

There are people who have

money and people who are rich

— Coco Chanel

THREE
WEALTH

The American Dream is a term that is often used but also often misunderstood. It isn't really about becoming rich or famous. It is about things much simpler and more fundamental than that.

— Marco Rubio
United States Senator for Florida

Each of us — wherever we are from, are now, or are going — has our own individual dream of living our life as it should be lived. What's yours?

Getting rich is a concept that goes back to the caveman days. And getting rich has its costs. In the 1994 movie *The Flintstones* Betty Rubble (played by Rosie O'Donnell) told Fred and Wilma Flintstone, "You used to be such nice people, but now... you're just a couple of rich snobs!"

People talk shit about "rich people" all the time without even trying to understand the concept of **wealth**. So in this chapter we're going to talk about the concept of **wealth**.

A Google search of "wealth" returned about 3,210,000,000 results in 0.69 seconds. And defines it **wealth** as "the state of being rich." A Google search of "rich" returned about 1,530,000,000 results in the same amount of time and defined rich as "having a great deal of money or assets, wealthy."

The American culture — and virtually every culture since the beginning of mankind —is crammed full of stories, legends, myths, fables, and dreams about wealth and riches.

As kids we hunted Easter eggs and played *Monopoly*. Rich people — and cartoon characters — pop up everywhere in our make-believe world. There's Richie Rich —the poor little rich boy — and Shirley Temple in the movie *Poor Little Rich Girl*. There's Mark Twain's novel *The Prince and the Pauper*.

There's Scrooge McDuck based on Charles Dickens' character Ebenezer Scrooge in his 1843 novella *A*

Christmas Carol. And there's another rich duck, his nephew Donald, who keeps more of a "millionaire next door" low profile.

Last but not least by any means are Gordon Gekko played by Michael Douglas in *Wall Street* (1987) and Jordan Belfort (a real person) played by Leonardo DiCaprio in *The Wolf of Wall Street* (2013).

Books are filled with stories about "rags to riches" like the ones created by Horatio Alger Jr. that had a major positive impact on America during *The Gilded Age* (1870-1900).

And almost everyone who dreams of getting rich has read — and reread — Napoleon Hill's 1937 iconic classic *Think and Grow Rich.*

Besides the make-believe millionaires our world has always been filled with real-time rich people. Let's jump into our time machine

First stop — King Solomon's Mines — 970 B.C. **King Solomon** was the last king of Israel and was said to have had 25 tons of gold.

Next to the Roman Empire around 50 B.C. to visit Emperor **Augustus Caesar** whose net worth might have been around $5 trillion in today's dollars.

Next to the Mongolian Empire around the late 1100's. **Genghis Khan** ruled over what might have been the largest physically connected empire in history and was possible worth trillions of dollars (with a T).

WEALTH

In Russia, **Tzar Nicholas**, before his untimely death in 1918, built an empire valued at hundreds of billions of dollars.

And we are going to visit West Africa in the 1300's. **Mansa Musa** — the King of Timbuktu. According to *Time* magazine "there was no way to put an accurate number on his wealth." But it is estimated that he was worth hundreds of billions of dollars.

These legendary fortunes were enormous because they were controlled by conquerors who grabbed whatever they could by force.

Back to modern times, let's visit some "Robber Barons" There's Henry Ford, Andrew Carnegie, Cornelius Vanderbilt and John D. Rockefeller. And legendary billionaires J. Paul Getty and Howard Hughes (played by Leonardo DiCaprio in the 2004 film — *The Aviator*) — were a different breed entirely.

So, what did we learn from our travels on the time machine? First is that rich people — rich people with a capital **"R"** as in **Rich** were *relatively* richer in the good old days. There will probably never be fortunes like those held by King Solomon, Augustus Caesar, Genghis Khan, Mansa Musa, and the Count of Monte Cristo.

However, the wealth amassed by some the 3,000 present day billionaires makes J. Paul Getty and Howard Hughes look poor. Same for many of the world's 50 million millionaires. What I mean is that wealth is relative. There will always be someone richer AND poorer than you.

WEALTH

Warren Buffet, Bill Gates, Jeff Bezos, Mark Zuckerberg, Elon Musk, Oprah Winfrey, Richard Branson and on and on — all living legends. And each one of them has their own story of their **Road to a Million or Billion.**

Our minds are bombarded with "rags to riches" stories. They are a dime a dozen and may not mean much to us because they are not us — and we are not them.

Having said that it's important for us to understand how wealth used to be accumulated — and how it is accumulated these days.

Like I said, there were the conquerors who did nothing to *create* wealth. They just grabbed what they could by any means possible (usually brute force) and help onto it as long as possible. This group includes the people we visited on our time machine trip as well as all the big names in ancient and modern history — let's just call them "The Bad Guys".

Then there were the "Robber Barons" who weren't much better by any means. They built massive fortune through exploiting others to their own advantage.

Howard Hughes — as wacky as he was — represented a new era of entrepreneurs. He was a pioneer in aviation and Hollywood and brought some added value to the game.

During the last half of the 1900's there were a lot of entrepreneur self-made millionaires whose names and companies and products we easily recognize.

WEALTH

There were the "Food Entrepreneurs": Ray Croc (McDonald's), Carl Karcher (Carl's Jr.), John Galardi (Wienerschnitzel), Glen Bell (Taco Bell), Verne Winchell (Winchell's Donuts) and so many others.

Now there are the "Sports and Entertainment" millionaires and billionaires including names like Gordon Ramsay, Oprah, J Lo, Jay Z, Magic Johnson, and — yes — even Snoop Dogg.

And speaking of Snoop Dogg we have "Cannabis Entrepreneurs" who are becoming multi-millionaires faster than Tuna in *Blow* (2001).

Everyone wants to be a millionaire and 50 million people have joined that not-so-elite club. I say that because lots of millionaires are making bank in illegal drugs, porn, human-trafficking, prostitution, and other industries out of the pay grade of this book. But there are enough legal ways to get there.

So, what are the legal (and realistic) ways to make bank (AKA get cheddar) in today's **C19 Economy**? There are five distinct — but not necessarily mutually exclusive — **Roads to a Million** and here they are.

1. **Earn Money by Working and Saving**
   This is the most common, the hardest, and usually the slowest (unless you have the talent to demand a big annual guaranteed salary and mega-bonuses). If you are a cardio-thoracic surgeon, successful hip-hop artist, or major league pitcher this is probably your **Road to a Million.** If you are "Joe the Plumber" or ask "do you want fries with that" at your job — it's *probably* not going to work for you.

2. **Inherit It or Marry It**
If you have rich parents or a rich uncle or a trust fund, you're all set — pass GO and collect $200 or $200 million. Remember what **Teflon Tim** once said: "You can marry more money in 5 minutes than you can make in a lifetime. But keep in mind that inherited wealth may give you the "things" you want — but does not guarantee the **LIFE** you want

3. **Invest in "The Market" Successfully**
   That's what I'm talking about — this is what this book — **Henry Park's Road to a Million** and my weekly **Zoom** classes are all about. We are investing in **Stocks, Bonds,** and **Alternative Investments.**

4. **Invest in Real Estate**
   Some people include **Real Estate** in the Alternative Investment category — I put it in a category by itself. Real Estate Investments can include Residential, Commercial, and Global.

5. **Start or Buy a Business**
   We've already seen that Entrepreneurship and Business Ownership can be a **Road to a Million** — but they can also lead to a major disaster and wipe you out in a nanosecond. So, **caveat emptor** — think about what you are doing and *why* before you jump into the **Shark Tank** or you may find yourself in *Hell's Kitchen*. One hint, lots of Baby Boomers are looking for exit strategies so there are some great companies out there that can be acquired at a discount.

These are NOT uncertain times, and we are NOT all in this together. These are very certain times. The certainty is that the world has been turned upside down and that it will probably remain upside down for a long, long, time — if not forever. And nothing could be farther from the truth about "we're all in this together." The pandemic has created MONSTERS and to say that it's a "dog-eat-dog" world is putting it mildly.

Last year (July 2020) — a few months after we started washing our hands **ad nauseum** and covering our faces with **do rags** and **gang bandanas** — I published a book titled **C19 Economics: Your Guide to Personal and Business Finance**. A homework assignment for you is to read my book and learn about the challenges and opportunities of the pandemic economy.

There has never been an economy like the one we have now. Believe me there are opportunities of a lifetime in **Investments, Real Estate**, and **Business**. These are the most exciting times of my life. What I mean is that I have entered a lot of races, always crossed the finish line, and have all of the T-shirts to prove it — but this is IT!

If you can't become a multi-millionaire in the next few years, I don't know what to tell you. Okay, before you throw this book in the trash let me explain what I mean. My personal goal is to show you how to make $1,000,000. Let me be perfectly clear. You are *investing* the money on your own — in your own account and in your own name.

I have written and published this book to get you started on your own **Road to a Million**. I don't want or need your money. I have plenty of my own and am making more all of the time. And it's not being made from books, seminars, podcasts, or webinars. I don't have a swimming pool or a Ferrari. I am not a guru or motivational speaker. I am just a guy who grew up in the barrio (Hawaiian Gardens is the smallest city in the County of Los Angeles) as a poor Korean kid who all the homeboys thought was a crazy rich Asian. That really messed with my mind — and still does. I was the kid who was working in the cafeteria for my free lunch while they were wearing designer shoes.

Maybe, like me, you grew up dreaming of being a millionaire — I did it. You're next!

The only thing standing between you and your goal is your bullshit story you keep telling yourself as to why you can't achieve it.

— Jordan Belfort (Leonardo DiCaprio)
The Wolf of Wall Street (2013)

FOUR

I know the difference
between black magic and
white magic.

— Tina Turner

FOUR
WALL STREET MAGIC

For twenty dollars I can tell you a lot of things. For thirty dollars I can tell you more. And for fifty dollars I can tell you everything.

— Madam Ruby (Erica Yohn)
Pee-wee's Big Adventure (1985)

These days the term **Wall Street** refers to more than the section of NYC where the New York Stock Exchange is located. It's an umbrella term that refers to all of the financial markets in the United States.

WALL STREET MAGIC

Wall Street is the most magical place in the world — more magical than the Sleeping Beauty Castle at Disneyland, a Vegas show of David Copperfield or Penn and Teller, or the Griffith Park Observatory Planetarium all rolled into one.

Working on Wall Street is like falling down Alice's Rabbit Hole, skipping down the Yellow Brick Road, and waking up in the Twilight Zone all at the same time. Pure magic! But Wall Street is, in many ways, still a private club where there are players and "play-az" — roles that are continually changing.

As a Mortgage Banker Wall Street is my world — and it has been my world for most of my career. Wall Street is alluring and addicting — it is fueled by both hype and hyperbole — and can be both sweet and sour at the same time.

In case you haven't seen Eddie Murphy as Billy Ray Valentine in *Trading Places* (1983), here's what I mean by sweet and sour at the same time:
Okay. Pork belly prices have been dropping all morning, which means that everybody's waiting for it to hit rock bottom so they can buy cheap and go long. Which means that the people who own the pork belly contracts are goin' bat shit. They're saying, 'Hey, we're losing all our goddam money, and Christmas is coming around the corner, and I ain't gonna have no money to buy my son the G.I. Joe with the kung-fu grip, right? And my wife won't f... my wife won't make love to me 'cuz I ain't got no money, right?' So they're panicking right now, and they're screaming 'SELL!' 'SELL!' to get out before the price keeps dropping. They're panicking out there right now! I can feel it! They out there!

Here are more movies about Wall Street:

Wall Street	1987
Glengarry Glen Ross	1992
Barbarians at the Gate	1993
Liar's Poker	1999
American Psycho	2000
Boiler Room	2000
Margin Call	2011
The Pit	2009
Wall Street: Money Never Sleeps	2010
Chasing Madoff	2010
The Flaw	2011
Goldman Sachs: Master of the World?	2011
Margin Call	2011
Arbitrage	2012
The Wolf of Wall Street	2013
How to Be a Billionaire	2014
The Big Short	2015
All Wars Are Bankers' Wars	2016
The Wizard of Lies	2017
Inside Lehman Brothers	2019

You can watch these movies, or you can read this book, join my **Facebook Group**, and attend my online classes on **Zoom** — and I will teach you more than you need to know.

Now I am going to share **My 13 Magic Tricks** based on my experience on **Wall Street** and provide you all the tools you need to succeed on your **Road to a Million.** Remember that no two **Roads to a Million** are even remotely identical and are rarely even similar. What I am saying is that I am going to give you the tools — the rest is up to you.

Where is the Wall Street Magic for you? (Draw your response.)

1
KNOWLEDGE

K nowledge is POWER. The more you learn about the economy, the markets, target companies, and investments in your portfolio the more successful you will be. Do not waste time on social media that you could be investing in yourself and your investment knowledge — the highest possible ROI is investing in yourself.

Beware of books, courses, seminars, and webinars that have one objective — to fuck you out of your money!

2
TIMING

Timing is EVERYTHING. Remember that you're never able to time the top or the bottom of the market — but you have to be able to maximize your return on trades and get as much out of the middle as you can.

Remember that when you think it's the right time to buy someone things it's the right time to sell and vice versa.

3

KARMA

K arma can be a bitch — or it can be a blessing. What I mean is that every trade has an opposite side. If you are buying someone is selling. If you are selling someone is buying. Put yourself in the mind of the matching trader and figuring out **why** they are doing what they are doing — and **why** you are doing what you are doing.

Think about buying a used car. Why is the other person selling it? And why are you buying it? A willing buyer and a willing seller strike a deal.

4
PRACTICE

There is no practice in investing. Either you pull the trigger, or you don't. Forget about trading games and paper portfolios. That's like playing cards for "fun". If you want to play cards for fun, then play a game of Crazy 8's or Go Fish. If you want to play poker like the big boys and girls then step up and put skin in the game.

Replace practice with EXPERIENCE. Experience is going to make you a winning investor.

5
DISCIPLINE

The **X-Factor** in investing is **DISCIPLINE**. Some have it — most don't. Investing can be like eating that bag of Kettle® Brand Hot! Jalapeño Potato Chips — you have to know when to stop munching. And sometimes you just need to know when to toss it into the trash and forget about it.

Just like in the song by one-hit wonder Meghan Trainer sings "'bout the base, no treble" — investing is all about DISCIPLINE.

6
FOCUS

E ver wonder why a racehorse wears blinders (and it's not by choice)? Blinders limit a horse's peripheral (side vision) forcing it to look forward toward the finish line. Focus on your or forget about getting rich and work at Carl's Jr.® where you can check Facebook in between asking customers "¿quires el combo?"

**Don't take your eyes off the Road to a Million —
remain laser focused.**

7
TECHNOLOGY

W hen I started on **Wall Street** technology was relatively in the Dark Ages compared to today. I spent tens of thousands of dollars for tools and information that is available at an exceptionally low cost (and sometimes at no cost) to everyone with a computer or smartphone. Invest in the best technology and make sure you leverage it.

Technology can be your best friend — or worst enemy. Invest in the best and use it wisely.

8
LEGENDS

H eroes and Villains — that's what Wall Street is all about. And be prepared for heroes to become villains as fast as a trade is electronically executed on an exchange — in less than a nanosecond. Warning — don't put much stock in today's "Wolves of Wall Street" because tomorrow they may be playing chess with Bernie.

Did Gordon Gekko's quote in *Wall Street* (1987) – "Greed, for lack of a better word, is good" — make him a hero or a villain?

9
MYTHS

M ore than any other place on earth — Wall Street is full of myths. All those bullshit stories people make up about how they timed the market perfectly or "discovered" a company that "nobody knew about". Yeah, some stories are true but *caveat emptor*.

The biggest myths on Wall Street are that you need an MBA or have to "know someone".

10
MONSTERS

We all have our own monsters somewhere in the back of our minds. Don't let your monsters destroy you from within. Your monsters can include everything from bad people to bad trades. Keep your monsters from fucking with your head.

FOMO — Fear of Missing Out — is a monster that can fuck with your mind.

11
BELIEF

From *Peter Pan* by J.M. Barrie (1914): **"The moment you doubt you can fly, you cease for ever to be able to do it."** To become a millionaire, you have to believe that you can become a millionaire. And that's all I have to say about that!

Believe in yourself, believe in God (whatever you believe your God to be), and hopefully believe in *Henry Park's Road to a Million*.

12
COURAGE

Believe it or not — courage comes in all sizes, colors, and flavors. You need courage to become a millionaire, but you won't find it skipping down the Yellow Brick Road with Dorothy, Toto, the Scarecrow, and the Tin Man singing "Lions and tigers and bears — oh my!" **It's in your heart not in the Land of Oz.**

Do you identify more with the Cowardly Lion or with Oz the Great and Powerful?

13
BLACK MAGIC

Almost everybody who's anybody has sang the iconic song *That Old Black Magic* (1942 — music by Harold Arlen and lyrics by Johnny Mercer). And there's a reason, we all love "that old black magic" — it's what makes Wall Street so damn alluring.

Alchemy, black shamanism, Voodoo, Macumba — do you believe in Black Magic?

The two words **Wall Street** conjure us as many different visions as there are stars in the sky.

Many people think of Rich Uncle Pennybags aka **Mr. Monopoly** — the round-man mascot of the board game wearing a big shit eating grin, a moustache, a morning suit with a bowtie, and a top hat.

Big time posers — you know the type — puff on cigars because they believe that's what millionaires do. People love to imitate millionaires buy most people don't even know what it's like to me a millionaire because they have never had **$1,000,000** or greater net worth (outside of their primary residence). There are "paper millionaires" and there are "liquid millionaires" and they are far from the same animal.

Read *The Millionaire Next Door: The Surprising Secrets of America's Wealthy* by Thomas J. Stanley and William D. Danko. Published in 1996, it Is still relevant and explains why not all millionaires have mansions with swimming pools, have private jets, and drive Bentleys. Not all millionaires smoke cigars or look like **Mr. Monopoly.**

When the Dutch controlled New York ("New Amsterdam") the street was known as de Waalstraat and there was a wall built along the street to protect the colonists from Native Americans.

In the 1700's traders and speculators gathered around a buttonwood to trade securities. That was the beginning of the New York Stock Exchange. Maybe youyou have visited Wall Street and looked down on the floor of the NYSE! It's a great experience not just the first time — every time.

So, you see Wall Street is a storied and magical place to many of us. To others it conjures up nightmares of **capitalist pigs** and everything that is believed to be bad about America's history — like conflicts with Native Americans and the slave market that existed there in the 1600's and 1700's.

You can make Wall Street whatever you want it to be — good, bad, ugly, or even magical.

Wall Street
is the only place
that people
ride to in a
Rolls Royce
to get advice from
those who take
the subway.

— Warren Buffett

FIVE

In any investment, you expect to have fun and make money.

— Michael Jordan

FIVE
INVESTMENT VEHICLES

Do not buy the hype from Wall St. and the press that stocks always go up. There are long periods when stocks do nothing, and other investments are better.

— Jim Rogers

The World of Investments encompasses so much more than stocks and bonds — different investment vehicles have different risks and rewards.

- Stocks
- Bonds
- Mutual Funds
- ETFs
- CEFs
- Hedge Funds
- Crypto
- Commodities
- Annuities
- Collectibles
- Precious Metals
- Real Estate
- Business Ownership
- Alternative Investments
- Forex
- Options
- Weird Stuff

H ave you watched the 1956 movie *Around the World in Eighty Days* (or the 2004 version)? Or read the novel by French author Jules Verne published in 1873?

Around the World in Eighty Days is the story of Londoner Phileas Fogg and his newly employed French valet Passepartout. Fogg bets his friends $2,000,000 that he can circumnavigate the globe in 80 days. To win the bet Fogg engages just about every form of transportation from camels to trains and from hot air balloons to boats.

As you begin your voyage on **Henry Park's Road to a Million** open your mind to all types of investment vehicles. Choose and use the best vehicle for each unique circumstance. Make your selection based achieving the least amount of risk and the lowest cost that will get you to your next destination in the least amount of time.

One final note of advice — do your homework. Each week I cover a different type of investment and various investment strategies on my **Friday Zoom at 5:00 PM (Pacific).— Meeting ID 589 380 4727.**

STOCKS

S tocks are a type of investments which are called **securities**. Stocks indicate ownership and are also called **equities**. Stocks represent a claim on the proportional share of a company's assets and profits as determined by the number of shares you own divided by the number of outstanding shares the company has issue. **Common shares** have voting rights, but **preferred shares** have a preference on dividends. People who own shares in a company are called **stockholders** or **shareholders**.

Stocks are traded worldwide on stock exchanges or **stock markets**. Those stocks are called **publicly traded stocks**. There are many types of stocks: **Blue Chip** (large, profitable companies), **Small Cap, Foreign, Speculative, Value, Growth, Income, Penny Stocks** — and stocks in privately-held companies.

STOCKS

Instructions: Let's get's some information about YOU and **STOCKS**. What's your level of experience? Do you own STOCKS now? If so, which ones? How do you **FEEL** about STOCKS as a vehicle on your **ROAD TO A MILLION**?

101

BONDS

Bonds are **debt securities** issued for one year or longer by corporations, governments, or agencies to raise capital by borrowing money. A bond, like a IOU, is a promise to repay the principal (amount borrowed) along with interest at a specified interest rate on a specific date. Some bonds do not pay interest, but all bonds require repayment of principal.

Most bonds are issued with a nominal face value and a coupon which is a percentage of the nominal value.

There are **Corporate Bonds, U.S. Government Bonds** (Treasuries), and **Municipal Bonds** (issued by state and local governments).

Bonds can be purchased directly from the issuers — and on the **secondary market.** A bond's price rises as its yield falls and vice versa.

BONDS

Instructions: Let's get's some information about YOU and **BONDS**. What's your level of experience? Do you own BONDS? If so, which ones? How do you **FEEL** about BONDS as a vehicle on your **ROAD TO A MILLION**?

MUTUAL FUNDS

A **Mutual Fund** is an investment company that raises money from shareholders to invest in stocks, bonds, options, commodities, money market securities, or other investment vehicles.

These are traditional open-ended funds that continue to allow money to come in (and out) of the investment pool. Mutual fund shares can be redeemed at NAV (Net Asset Value) the close of any trading day.

- Priced once a day at 4:00 PM (Eastern)
- Purchase accessibility varies
- Portfolio transparency is **low**
- There are **no** listed options
- They are continually offered for sale
- Actively managed by professionals
- They have expense rations and, typically, fee schedules

MUTUAL FUNDS

Instructions: Let's get's some information about YOU and the **MUTUAL FUNDS**. What's your level of experience? Do you own MUTUAL FUNDS now? If so, which ones? How do you **FEEL** about MUTUAL FUNDS as a vehicle on your **ROAD TO A MILLION**?

ETFs

Exchange Traded Funds (ETFs) are a lot like a stock — you can set limit orders, short the shares and buy them on margin. The capital structure of ETFs is not closed. ETFs are actively managed and most of them track the performance of an investment index.

ETFs cannot issue debt or preferred shares and are designed to shield investors from capital gains much better than open-end funds or closed end funds.

- Priced intraday
- High portfolio transparency
- Listed options
- Continually offered
- Passive management
- Underlying portfolio of investments with a net asset value (NAV)

ETFs

Instructions: Let's get's some information about YOU and **ETFs**. What's your level of experience? Do you own ETFs now? If so, which ones? How do you **FEEL** about ETFs as a vehicle on your **ROAD TO A MILLION**?

CEFs

Closed-end Funds (CEFs) issue a fixed number of shares which are usually traded on a stock exchange. The share price is determined by the market and may represent either more (a premium) or less (a discount) to the net asset value (NAV) of the underlying investments in the fund.

Closed-end funds share some things with traditional (open-ended) mutual funds and ETFs — but there are also major differences.

- Professionally managed actively
- Have expense ratios and, typically, fee schedules
- May offer distribution of income and capital gains to investors
- Trade during the day on exchanges
- Can set limit orders, short the shares, and buy on margin
- Portfolios may be leverage

Instructions: Let's get's some information about YOU and **CEFs**. What's your level of experience? Do you own CEFs now? If so, which ones? How do you **FEEL** about CEFs as a vehicle on your **ROAD TO A MILLION**?

HEDGE FUNDS

Hedge Funds are designed to use non-traditional investment strategies to generate higher-than-normal investment returns by using tactics like short selling, program trading, risk arbitrage, leverage — and tools like futures, options, and derivative securities.

Hedge funds get their name from the term **hedging** which refers to actions taken to protect the value of an investment portfolio from market changes — often offsetting risk exposure by entering an offsetting position having the exact opposite pay-off pattern.

Hedge fund managers utilize numerous complex strategies to reduce risk — and aggressively to speculate in a market. To learn more about the World of Wall Street and, specifically, hedge funds, watch the series *Billions* on Amazon Prime Video.

HEDGE FUNDS

<u>Instructions:</u> Let's get's some information about YOU and **HEDGE FUNDS**. What's your level of experience? Do you own HEDGE FUNDS now? If so, which ones? How do you **FEEL** about HEDGE FUNDS as a vehicle on your **ROAD TO A MILLION**?

CRYPTO

C ryptocurrency also known as crypto currency or simply crypto is a digital asset. Crypto is designed as a digital currency that can be used to buy and sell goods and services using cryptography to secure online transactions. Cryptography makes it almost impossible to counterfeit or double spend. Many cryptos are virtual currencies using blockchain technology — a decentralized network of computers.

Bitcoin is the most widely recognized cryptocurrency, but others include **Dogecoin** and **Coinbase** which I have explained on my Zoom Classes. **BTFD** (Buy the Fucking Dip).

Allison Morrow published *A beginner's guide to crypto lingo* on *CNN Business* (April 26, 2021). Here's the URL: https://www.cnn.com/2021/04/26/investing/crypto-definitions/index.html

CRYPTO

Instructions: Let's get's some information about YOU and **CRYPTO**. What's your level of experience? Do you own CRYPTO now? If so, which ones? How do you **FEEL** about CRYPTO as a vehicle on your **ROAD TO A MILLION**?

COMMODITIES

The best explanation of **commodities** comes from *Trading Places* (1983):

Now what are commodities? Commodities are agricultural products... like coffee you had for breakfast... wheat, which is used to make bread... pork bellies, which is used to make bacon, which you might find in a bacon, lettuce and tomato sandwich. And then there are other commodities, like frozen orange juice... and GOLD. Though, of course, gold doesn't grow on trees like oranges... Now some of our clients are speculating that the price of gold will rise in the future. And we have clients who are speculating that the price of gold will fall.

Commodities are grouped into three categories: **Agriculture, Energy,** and **Metals** and are traded globally as publicly traded tangible assets. Investors can own commodities outright or buy options on commodities futures contracts. There are also commodities-related stocks and funds.

COMMODITIES

<u>Instructions:</u> Let's get's some information about YOU and **COMMODITIES**. What's your level of experience? Do you own COMMODITIES now? If so, which ones? How do you **FEEL** about COMMODITIES as a vehicle on your **ROAD TO A MILLION**?

ANNUITIES

Annuities are like IOUs. They are contracts designed to provide regular payments to policyholders in return for an initial lump sum investment. Annuities may have a guaranteed period and/or have payments for life. The payments may be a fixed amount or vary. Annuities are widely used as a means of generating guaranteed cash flow during retirement years

There are **fixed annuities** which are guaranteed by their issuers and are like a certificate of deposit but on a tax-deferred basis until payments begin. **Equity-indexed annuities** are a type of tax-deferred annuity whose credited interest is linked to an index like the S&P 500. **Equity-indexed annuities** are hybrids of fixed and variable annuities. **Variable annuities** are tax deferred and allow you to select from several investments — annuity payments depend on portfolio return.

ANNUITIES

Instructions: Let's get's some information about YOU and the **ANNUITIES**. **What's** your level of experience? Do you own ANNUITIES now? If so, which ones? How do you **FEEL** about ANNUITIES as a vehicle on your **ROAD TO A MILLION**?

COLLECTIBLES

Collectables refer to items that are currently worth (or perceived to be) more than they originally cost because of their rarity or popularity. Remember the Cabbage Patch Doll Craze? Collectables include **antiques, toys, coins, comic books, baseball cards, stamps,** and **wine**. I am also going to include **Fine Art** (at the risk of anyone who might have majored in Fine Art at UCI — you know who you are).

Investing in collectibles may include considerable risks, costs, and fees. Also, there is the possibility of counterfeits and the possibility of the destruction or damage to the property. There is no investment income, dividends, or capital gain realization until the assets are sold.

Benefits include diversification and long-term appreciation. Liquidity may be a problem.

COLLECTIBLES

<u>Instructions:</u> Let's get's some information about YOU and **COLLECTIBLES**. What's your level of experience? Do you own COLLECTIBLES now? If so, which ones? How do you **FEEL** about COLLECTIBLES as a vehicle on your **ROAD TO A MILLION**?

PRECIOUS METALS

Precious Metals are rare metals that high monetary value, including: **gold, silver, platinum, palladium,** and **copper**. Investing in precious metals can be a great way to diversify and hedge against inflation.

There are many ways to invest in precious metals in addition to the physical assets — like gold bullion — (bars and coins). There are certificates for those who do not want to take physical delivery of precious metals.

You can invest in stocks, mutual funds, and ETFs. Futures and options offer leverage for those who can stomach higher risk in pursuit of higher returns.

You can also invest in a gold, silver, or copper mine from one of emails you receive along with the ones from the Nigerian Minister of Finance. Read Harry Dent's newsletter.

PRECIOUS METALS

Instructions: Let's get's some information about YOU and **PRECIOUS METALS**. What's your level of experience? Do you own PRECIOUS METALS now? If so, which ones? How do you **FEEL** about PRECIOUS METALS as a vehicle on your **ROAD TO A MILLION**?

REAL ESTATE

Real Estate includes property in land, buildings, or housing, as distinct from personal property (physical property). Types of real estate include residential, **commercial**, **investment**, **luxury**, and **global**.

Investing in real estate involves purchasing, owning, managing, renting and/or selling of real estate for profit or income. Residential and commercial development is a sub-specialty of real estate investing along with distressed properties, flipping, foreclosures, and some others.

This is a hot time for real estate investing in the **commercial** and **global** arenas. The pandemic has created — and will continue to create tremendous opportunities for seasoned and talented real estate investors. If you are a newbie, caveat emptor, it's not as easy as the informercials want you to believe.

REAL ESTATE

<u>Instructions:</u> Let's get's some information about YOU and the **REAL ESTATE**. What's your level of experience? Do you own Investment REAL ESTATE now (do not include your Primary Residence)? If so, which ones? How do you FEEL about REAL ESTATE as a vehicle on your **ROAD TO A MILLION**?

BUSINESS OWNERSHIP

Owning a Business, for some, is as much a part of the American Dream as McDonald's, apple pie, and owning a house.

People start or buy businesses for a variety of reasons — and they all don't get rich. In fact, making a business profitable is something that very few people do.

A business may provide you with income — hopefully enough — but think long and hard whether the business can create wealth.

Pursue your passion but think about the best place you can leverage your time and money. Buy an undervalued or underperforming business and turn it around and sell it you might be able to make some coin. If you like baking, then bake some cookies but don't count on becoming another(Wally) Famous Amos.

BUSINESS OWNERSHIP

Instructions: Let's get's some information about YOU and **BUISNESS OWNERSHIP**. What's your level of experience? Do you an interest in a BUSINESS now? If so, which business(es)? Are you planning to buy or start a BUSINESS? How do you FEEL about BUSINESS OWNERSHIP as a vehicle on your **ROAD TO A MILLION**?

ALTERNATIVE INVESTMENTS

Alternative Investments include those that cannot be described as vanilla — like stocks and bonds. We have already covered commodities, collectibles, and hedge funds but here are some other alternative investments.

There are distressed securities, exchange funds, carbon credits, precious stones, and investments in mining, forestry, and film production — among other alternative investments.

Access to alternative investments comes through equity hedge funds, crowdfunding, private equity, and venture capital.

Alternative investments are typically brought into investment portfolios for diversification and in pursuit of higher returns. Keep in mind that these usually involve higher risk.

Instructions: Let's get's some information about YOU and **ALTERNATIVE INVESTMENTS**. What's your level of experience? Do you own ALTERNATIVE INVESTMENTS now? If so, which ones? How do you FEEL about ALTERNATIVE INVESTMENTS as a vehicle on your **ROAD TO A MILLION**?

FOREX

Foreign Exchange is also known as **forex**. To trade forex, you invest in foreign currency like you invest in stocks, bonds, or mutual funds. The difference is that instead of hoping to earn a profit through a price increase in the value of your investment, you hope that your position will either go up — or go down against the value of the U.S. Dollar. If you call it right, you make money. If you're wrong you lose money. When your foreign currency moves in the direction that you had hoped for then you convert it into U.S. Dollars and earn your profit.

Create a **forex strategy**, pick your pairs (foreign currency + U.S. Dollar), and select your asset class — options or futures.

You must stay on top of your forex positions because currencies move much faster than most stocks.

Instructions: Let's get's some information about YOU and **FOREIGN CURRENCIES**? What's your level of experience? Do you own FOREIGN CURRENCIES now? If so, which ones? How do you FEEL FOREIGN CURRENCIES as a vehicle on your **ROAD TO A MILLION**?

OPTIONS

O ptions are a right, but not an obligation, to buy or sell a specific security at an agreed price within an agreed **time** period. Options are all about time and that's why you see an alarm clock icon at the top of this page.

Call options give the purchaser the right, but not the obligation, to buy an investment asset on or before an agreed upon date (known as the option expiration date). That is the way it works with American calls. In Europe options can only be exercised **on** the expiration date (not before). **Put options** give the purchaser, but not the obligation, to sell an investment asset at an agreed price or on an agreed date (Europe) or before an agreed date (America).

Options offer many strategic alternatives and have the potential to deliver higher returns that investing in the underlying stocks.

OPTIONS

Instructions: Let's get's some information about YOU and the **OPTIONS**. What's your level of experience? Do you own RETIREMENT ACCOUNTS? If so, where are they invested? How do you FEEL about OPTIONS as a vehicle on your **ROAD TO A MILLION**?

WEIRD STUFF

Weird Stuff may include **lean hogs, vintage wines, classic cars,** and **contemporary art.** Your kid's lemonade stand doesn't fall under this category —nor does selling ecstasy at a rave or a loose joint at a concert.

Investing in your brother-in-law's "Sushi Wow" franchise probably comes under the "weird stuff" category — not because it's sushi but because it's your brother-in-law. You might as well give him the money because you'll probably never see it again.

In the final analysis you can invest in bull sperm, a Mexican restaurant, 18 timeshares, or whatever makes you happy. There are different reasons for making investments —and it's always about the highest ROI or lowest risk. Invest wisely but have fun doing it because after all it's your money Investing in **weird stuff** can be a lot of fun.

Instructions: Let's get's some information about YOU and the **WEIRD STUFF**. What's the weirdest investment you have ever made or have had presented to you?

To be a successful business owner and investor, you have to be emotionally neutral to winning and losing. Winning and losing are just part of the game.

— Robert Kiyosaki

SIX

If you don't know where you're

going, any road will get you there.

— Lewis Carroll

SIX
TRAVEL OPTIONS

Travel isn't always pretty. It isn't always comfortable. Sometimes it hurts, it even breaks your heart. But that's OK. The journey changes you; it should change you. It leaves marks on your memory, on your consciousness, on your heart, and on your body. You take something with you. Hopefully, you leave something good behind.

— Anthony Bourdain

Sixteen months before he died Anthony Bourdain was featured in an article in *The New Yorker* titled "Anthony Bourdain's Moveable Feast: Guided by a lusty appetite for indigenous culture and cuisine, the swaggering chef has become a travelling statesman." (by Patrick Radden Keefe – February 5, 2017). In the article Bourdain is quoted as saying: **"I travel around the world, eat a lot of shit, and basically do whatever the fuck I want."**

Anthony Bourdain's **Road to a Million** was a rocky one that ultimately led to death by a drug overdose at age 61. It was a premature ending for a man who lived an amazing life that was indeed a "moveable feast." A homework assignment for you to *Google* "Anthony Bourdain" and read about his life, books, adventures, business ventures and particularly his investments and personal finances. You may be surprised — but then again — maybe not. So why did I share that? Please read (or re-read the quote on the previous page and then think about Bourdain's summary of his life: **"I travel around the world, eat a lot of shit, and basically do whatever the fuck I want."**

Forget about Bourdain's **Road to a Million** and think about your own — and only your own.

At the beginning of this book, I asked you: "What is the most important thing in your life?" To choose the right travel options for your **Road to a Million** you MUST honestly answer that question.

You're about to learn about four travel options: **DIY, Mass Transit, Charter,** and **Henry Park's Party Bus**. Hopefully, after weighing all of the options, you will jump on my party bus so **we can travel around the world, eat a lot of shit, and do whatever the fuck we want while getting rich at the same time.**

Remember Jules Verne's *Around the World in Eighty Days*? Phileas Fogg took advantage of all classes of **investment vehicles** and all **travel options. DIY** is Drive It Yourself which can be a tough way to go with lots of speed bumps, road hazards, and roadblocks. **Mass Transit** includes all types of professionally managed funds with pooled money. **Charter** relates to privately managed funds. And you'll learn about my party bus when you jump on.

DIY

If everything seems under control, you're just not going fast enough.

— Mario Andretti

When the dot com companies were blowing up NASDAQ back in the day it seemed like everyone became a self-proclaimed **Day Trader.** And what happened to all those day traders when they blew through their savings and retirement.

Go direct to Henry Park's Party Bus, do not pass GO, but you can collect $2,000,000.

146

MASS TRANSIT

The mutual fund industry has been built, in a sense, on witchcraft.

— John C. Bogle
Founder of the Vanguard Group

Mass Transit includes funds where your money is pooled with other people's money and managed by an investment company — includes mutual funds, hedge funds, and managed retirement accounts (401k).

Keep in mind that it may be hard to outperform most professional money managers — but it can be done.

147

CHARTER

The "know nothing" investor should practice diversification, but it's crazy if you are an expert.

— Charlie Munger

Charter is like traveling in a private jet with your own personal pilot. Most ballers who don't have the time or inclination to manage their own investments have their own investment advisor.

Investment Advisors who manage private money must be registered with their respective states and/or SEC.

HENRY PARK'S PARTY BUS

Going so soon? I wouldn't hear of it. Why my little party's just beginning.

— Wicked Witch of the West
Wizard of Oz (1939)

My **Party Bus** ma be your best travel option because you can do whatever you want. You'll learn how to be **your own portfolio manager.**

Picking stocks and bonds is the easy part — knowing when to buy and when to sell them is the magic.

149

Capitalism tries for a delicate balance: it attempts to work things out so that everyone gets just enough stuff to keep them from getting violent and trying to take other people's stuff.

— George Carlin

SEVEN

They don't like you but they will be checking your page religiously.
-Henry Park

SEVEN
YOUR ROAD TO A MILLION

Money is better than poverty, if only for financial reasons.

— Woody Allen

This chapter is all about you — I can lead a Capitalist Pig to the water, but I can't make it drink. Right now, make some initial notes about Your Road to a Million and come back and revisit until you have created a solid plan for your trip.

WTF?

Before you look through the next 11 pages and start wondering why they're all blank let me give you a heads-up. I could write **Your Road to a Million** but that would be like me having a ghostwriter write **Henry Park's Road to a Million.**

Here are 11 pages for you to create your own strategy for getting from $1,000 to a Million Dollars (or more). If you have $1,000,000 to start than maybe you can shoot for a Billion Dollars!

I have given you all the tools that you need in this book. All you have to keep on top of the market and investment opportunities is to join my Facebook Group — *Henry Park's Road to a Million* — and **participate** (the operative word) in my weekly **Zoom** classes every Friday at 4:00 PM (Pacific Time).

The operative word with this book, my Facebook group, my **Zoom** classes, and your **Road to a Million** is *participate*. Don't just browse half-ass through my book, lurk in my Facebook group, or log into my Zoom classes and hide with your video off — **participate!**

<u>Instructions:</u> This is **YOUR ROAD TO A MILLION.** The next 11 pages are BLANK — I have purposely left them blank because I want you to plan your own road trip based on the information I have shared with you so far in this book. Remember that it is a "work in progress" because you need to get on the road — we're burning daylight. So, pack your bags, fill up your tank (or charge up if you're driving a Tesla), grab some high energy snacks and beverages, set your navigation to destination **$1,000,000** and hit the road Jack (or Jill). This chapter is all about **YOU**.

Capitalism is an organized system to guarantee that greed becomes the primary force of our economic system and allows the few at the top to get very wealthy and has the rest of us riding around thinking we can get that way, too — if we just work hard enough, sell enough Tupperware and Amway products, we can get a pink Cadillac.

— Michael Moore

EIGHT

A Tail of Two Piggies

What do you see different about
the two piggies above?

I n early **Korea** pigs were associated with wealth. In many countries and cultures throughout history pigs are thought of as dirty animals and — more-than-often — pigs are associated with greed. In Korea pigs represent fertility and wealth. Many Koreans believe that dreaming of pigs is a sign that great riches will soon come to them. So, I hope that all of you reading this book will start dreaming of pigs tonight — **Big Fat Capitalist Pigs.**

The previous page has two pigs in my logo. What is different about the pigs? The pig on the left has his tail down. What does that mean? It means that he is a fucking loser and with that attitude has no chance in hell of ever becoming a millionaire. In fact, if he keeps his tail down some big hog is going to bite it off and he'll be tailless.

The pig on the right is a fucking baller. He not only has his tail pointing up but it's curled. That means he's confident and has no fear. Mexican pigs are thinking to themselves: "No tengo miedo pendejos."

Let's take a closer look at the science of pig body language and specifically **pig tail tells**.
- Tail down and between the legs = fearful of having his tail bitten off.
- Up in the air and flicking = alert.
- Tail curled = happy and positive.
- Down and motionless = depressed.
- Tail curled = happy and positive.
- Down and motionless = depressed.
- Loosely wagging = kick backed (*sus california*).

PIG TELLS

For more information about porcine body language and tells, you can read a 37-page paper by Jordy Groffen titled *"Tail posture and motion as a possible indicator of emotional state in pigs."* (2102.

In **Chinese culture** pigs represent luck, wealth, and prosperity. In China pigs enjoy a historical celebrity status because — in addition to luck, wealth, and prosperity — pigs represent growth and development.

So, what have you just learned? You need to keep your tail up and curled so you can be a **Badass Capitalist Pig**.

Now maybe you understand why chose a filthy animal for my **Road to a Million** logo.

EIGHT
ROADS NOT TAKEN

I shall be telling this with a sigh
Somewhere ages and ages hence:
Two roads diverged in a wood, and I —
I took the one less traveled by,
And that has made all the difference.

— Robert Frost
The Road Not Taken (1915)

Life — and investing — is all about choices. You come to a fork in the road and you turn left or you turn right. And life is sometimes more about The Roads Not Taken as it is about the roads that you choose to take.

O nce upon a time not so long ago or so very far away lived two brothers who happened to be pigs (literally).

Louie and Lucky were identical twins (yes, pigs can be identical twins) but DNA was about the only thing that they had in common besides being pigs. Well maybe not the only thing. They both were dreamers and wanted to get the hell out of the pig shit as quickly as possible. And neither of them wanted to end up as Organic Applewood Smoked Canadian Bacon at Whole Foods or a spiral-sliced ham at HoneyBaked.

So, one night they "flew the coop" or whatever pigs do — escape the pig pen? The years passed and the piglets grew into porkers. Louie believed that the **Road to a Million** was hard work while Lucky believed in working smart. They had quite different beliefs in how to achieve the American Dream but attended college together majoring in Business Administration. The years passed and birthdays came and went, and they got fatter and fatter. Here is their story — *A Tale of Two Piggies* — to the best of my memory when I heard it for the first time as a young man working on Wall Street.

After graduation Louie took a job in corporate America as a "Management Trainee" at a Fortune 500 Company with (what he though was) a fat salary, a 401k, stock options, and two weeks of paid vacation and another week of paid vacation with every more 10 years of "service". After 3 years he could become a "Sr. Manager" and then would get a car allowance and expense account. Louie couldn't believe how "lucky" he was. He thought he had died and already gone to "hog heaven." If he played his cards right, he could retire at 65 with a "good" pension on top of his Porcine Social Security Benefits.

Louie fell in love and married a figure skater and had three little piglets. They moved to the burbs and bought a house. Through the years Louie contributed to his 401k but never really did much more in the way of savings or investments. After all, with the mortgage, and car payments, and the timeshare he always seemed to be living check to check.

Eventually the figure skater got fat, much fatter than Louie, and he traded her in for a younger, sleeker model (yes, she was really a model of some kind or another). It was at nasty divorce that was a financial disaster for the family. For whatever reason(s) Louie lost his job, the piglets had to drop out of college, and the "model" had to get a sales job at Kohl's, and they put the family home on the market. After a while on unemployment a pandemic hit and Louie's hopes of finding a new job vaporized.

Without his Fortune 500 job Louie was lost. He felt betrayed. He had believed in the American Dream — he had bought into it 100%. #1 - go to college. #2 - get a "good" job. #3 - work hard. #4.- retire at 65. #5 – live the life. But the American Dream never came.

Sitting around home waiting for his unemployment check and worried about foreclosure Louie became very depressed. The piglets never came to visit — but why would they? Louie had always been working "too hard" to spend time with them. The model (Kohl's sales clerk) left him, and he sat at home alone drinking most nights with all the house lights left up bright.

ROADS NOT TAKEN

After graduation Lucky took off for Europe for "a few months" but didn't come home for a year. After those "few months" in Europe he traveled throughout South America on a motorcycle. Finally, he became a little homesick and returned to quickly find a job in "sales." It really didn't matter what he sold because Lucky was a "natural" — he was a sales wizard. During the year that he was traveling Lucky learned a lot about people. He learned what makes people happy — and what makes them unhappy. And he learned how to make money, lots of money, by making unhappy people happy.

Lucky wasn't called "Lucky" for nothing. At first, he was thought to be stillborn, but he was revived. He had anemia but he recovered. And he survived being attacked by a team of hogs. What made Lucky "lucky" was his *happy go lucky* attitude about life. Lucky did not believe in working "hard" — he believed in working "smart."

Lucky didn't want a corporate job like his brother Louie had. When Lucky returned from Europe and South America, he noticed how unhappy Louie had already become in his job. All Louie talked about was his job and he was working sixty hours a week, his 401k, and how he was going to retire to Florida *someday*. He never mentioned that that "someday" was at least forty years away. And he would not admit to himself or anyone else that his dream may never come true.

Lucky got a job selling life insurance and became a stockbroker and eventually a financial advisor. His earnings were entirely commissions earned on his own success. During his career he continually pivoted and reinvented himself. He fell in love, got married, and had two piglets. And because he believed in working smart instead of hard, he spent a lot of time with those piglets. In fact, Lucky's mantra was to build and protect as much personal wealth as he could by working as little as possible. There was more to Lucky's success than luck. It was mostly his attitude, his passion for life, and his commitment to being a "lifestyle ambassador" — that was his "why."

No two pigs are alike — even capitalist pigs from the same litter. But why did Louie and Lucky take two different roads in their lives? It all comes down to perspective and attitude. Louie believed in working "hard."

Lucky believed in working "smart." Louie worked to live, and Lucky lived to work (as little as possible and make as possible.

Louie and Lucky were born on a pig factory farm where the survival rate is low because of the sedentary and crowded conditions. If they would not have escaped, I would not be sharing their story. They might have become pork bellies like those traded in the 1983 Eddie Murphy movie *Trading Places.*

When the pandemic hit Louie froze like a pig in the headlights and became roadkill — the American Dream became the American Nightmare. He went from Hog Heaven to Hog Hell.

Lucky's perspective was one of more opportunity and he continued to live life to the fullest, enjoy his family. His income and wealth continued to grow astronomically because he invested in the **Road to a Million Fund.**

175

There's a lesson — or many lessons — somewhere is in story of *A Tail of Two Piggies*. If you're smart enough then you will think about why I have spent the last ten pages of this book talking about fucking pigs. Maybe it's that our attitudes and perspectives determine which road(s) we choose to take — or not to take — in our lives. And, consequently, — where we eventually end up (with or without our tails intact).

What roads have you NOT taken?

The woods are lovely, dark,
   and deep.
But I have promises to keep,
And miles to go before I sleep,
And miles to go before I sleep.

— Robert Frost
Stopping By Woods on a Snowy Evening (1923)

NINE

I have been trading for years and I am still standing. I have seen a lot of traders come and go. They have a system or a program that works in some specific environments and fails in others. In contrast, my strategy is dynamic and ever-evolving. I constantly learn and change.

— Thomas Busby

NINE
SERVICE RECORDS

Trading is a serious thing — or at least it should be. I have been trading for decades and decided to share *some* of my trades with my **Facebook Group** about a year ago. Keep in mind that I have a day job that involves trading bonds —and running a bunch of companies ® and that trade significantly in almost all markets and with almost all investment vehicles.

This chapter covers trades I shared in **Henry Park's Road to a Million** on Facebook which has grown to over 1,200 members since I started May 2, 2020. Keep in mind that they are trading their own money in their own trading accounts. I am suggesting trades but most people who participate in the group mirror my trades.

TRADE #1 $250 BUY BTC
TRADE #2 $250 BUY BTC
TRADE #3 SOLD $500 BTC
          FOR $590
TRADE #4 BUY $84 OF XLM
          WITH PROFITS
          (LESS COINBASE FEES)
          BALANCE: $1,000
TRADE # 5 BUY $922 OF FNMA *
          (PRICE OF $1.95)
TRADE #6 BUY $220 OF NRZ **
* $4 DOLLAR FOR TRANSACTION FEE
** $4 DOLLAR TRANSACTION FEE
TRADE # 7 SELL $840 OF FNMA
          (PRICE OF $2.10)

ACCOUNTING

TRADE #8 BUY 10 SHARES OF DKNG
          (PRICE OF $43.70)
TRADE #9 BUY 180 SHARES OF FNMA
          (PRICE OF $2.20)
TRADE #10 SELL 33 SHARES OF NRZ
          (PRICE OF $9.58)
TRADE #11 BUY 7 SHARES OF LUV
          (PRICE OF $54.59)
TRADE # 12 SELL 180 SHARES OF FNMA
          (PRICE OF $2.16)
TRADE # 13 SELL 10 SHARES OF DKNG
          (PRICE OF $39.50)

#14 BUY 32 SHARES OF AAL
          (PRICE OF $12.05)
#15 BUY 10 SHARES OF UAL
          (PRICE OF $58.43)
#16 SELL 7 SHARES OF LUV
          (PRICE OF $58.41)
#17 SELL 10 SHARES OF UAL
          (PRICE OF $45.05)
#18 SELL 32 SHARES OF AAL
          (PRICE OF $18.28)
19 BUY 5 SHARES OF NKLA
          (PRICE OF $82.74)

ACCOUNTING

TRADE #20 SELL 5 SHARES OF NKLA
          (PRICE OF $69.74)
TRADE #21 BUY 20 SHARES OF JFIN
          (PRICE OF $5.15)
TRADE #22 BUY 100 SHARES OF HTZ
          (PRICE OF $2.19)
TRADE #23 SELL 20 SHARES OF JFIN
          (PRICE OF $5.68)
TRADE #24 SELL 100 SHARES OF HTZ
          (PRICE OF $2.12)

CURRENT CASH BALANCE: $ 1,412.59
EQUITY: $ 1,412.59

182

Henry Park
June 15, 2020 · 🌐

Here is the most updated mark to market report including today's trades. I am currently flat on all positions. Get ready. The market is starting to act volatile. Remember bears 🐻 make money 📊 bulls make money. Pigs 🐷 get slaughtered. I am still up over 40% on my money!! When did we start like a month and a 1/2 ago? 😂.....also keep in mind the percentage of gain. We have been trading very safe. Not "ALL IN" like some people. If you go "ALL IN" you can double up real fast and get wiped out a few trades later. Don't pay attention to people who do that. On a side note 📝 I'm up huge on my personal accounts. Same trades just larger amounts. Just an FYI. **See Less**

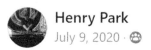

Henry Park
July 9, 2020 · 😊

Hip hip hooray!!! After today's sale of Tesla stock we are at $1,519.81. This is also assuming JFIN stock (which I'm still holding. I am valuing the stock at $4.00 for mark to market purposes) This means if you started with me with $1,000 you would have made a 51.9% ROI (return on investment). Formula: $519.81 / $1,000 = 51.9%

51.9% return on investment is not bad considering we started 2 months ago. May 2nd to be exact. That's when I started this club.

Now things are going to go faster and faster from here. Get ready. We will start learning more complex trades and I need you to pay attention.

So what have you learned so far ? Are you a better trader ? Do you know more about the stock market than 2 months ago ? Comment down below. **See Less**

Henry Park
August 3, 2020 · 😦

Here's the latest trade blotter......

Henry Park
September 1, 2020 ·

• • •

Here is my latest trade blotter. It took me forever to double the initial $1,000 we started with. It took 41 trades to get here. But if you have been following me as of today you should have DOUBLED your money. As of today I am at $2,299.41. Hopefully by now you have learned a few things. We learned a bunch of subject matter. We learned about Cryptocurrency. We learned about how to short. What makes stocks go up and what makes it go down. Now we are going to start learning stuff that is a little more complicated. But i will be there holding your hands every step of the way. **See Less**

Henry Park
September 8, 2020 · 🌐

With all the trades this morning here's the aftermath. 😆. It does seem like a lot but I had to make some major adjustments to protect the portfolio. We are in the midst of a market sell off in the Nasdaq. You don't want to be owning any Apple or Tesla right now. Stay away from tech stocks.

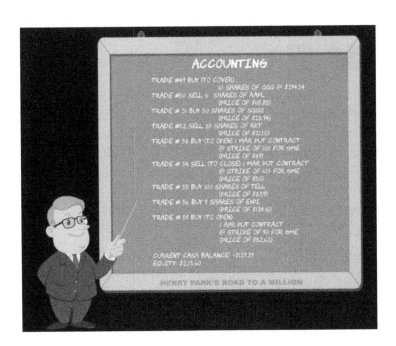

Henry Park
February 4 ·

· · ·

We started this group on May 2020. When i started i started with $1,000. Since then we've explored oil futures, cryptocurrency, how to trade options. We learned about charts and fundamental trading. We've made some good trades and some bad ones. But guess what?? We survived!! And if you traded right along side me you should have doubled your money by now. Especially with the last short on GameStop.

Not bad considering it hasn't even been a year yet. But one takeaway I want you to learn is this. Anything you want to be good at, you need to practice. Consistency is the key. Most people lose money because they either 1) Don't do their homework 2) Not being consistent 3) Gamble

What I am doing is not gambling. If it was, I would have lost a long time ago. You can't make almost 50 trades and only starting with $1,000 if it was and still live to tell the tale.

The capital markets is just that. It's a market to buy and sell. And if you are good at it you can make a fortune. **See Less**

Henry Park
April 5 at 2:31 PM · 😁   •••

If your in the group you will be happy to know that I started at $1,000 and as of now 10 months later I'm up over $4,000. $4,106.80 to be exact. 😄 400% Return on investment (ROI) isn't bad considering most hedge funds only return 20% on average. We still have one trade left which is BMBL. Can't win them all. I'm still holding on that for now. So let's be patient. I'm going to go hunting for the next good trade. ✌️

TRADES _____ — _____

TRADES _____ — _____

LEARNING HOW TO INVEST IS A LOT LIKE LEARNING TO RIDE A SKATEBOARD — YOU HAVE TO LEARN HOW TO BALANCE AND CONTROL YOUR SPEED — AND HOPE YOU DON'T TAKE ANY BAD SPILLS

TEN

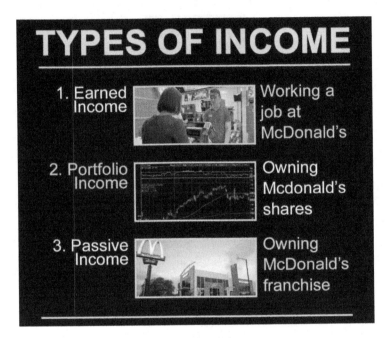

TEN
TOOLKIT

The best investment is in the tools of one's own trade.

— Benjamin Franklin

You are cordially invited to attend my weekly Zoom Classes on

INVESTING

Fridays — 5 PM (Pacific)
Meeting ID — 589 380 4727
(No password or secret handshake required.)

H ere are summaries of eighteen classes that I have taught since I started my **Henry Park's Road to a Million** *Facebook Group* and *Zoom Classes*. More are coming.

NYSE

NASDAQ

DOW JONES

STANDARD & POOR'S 500

DAX

BUY OR SELL? STOCK MARKET

TRADING OPTIONS

PRE-IPO STOCKS

CHARTS

JAPANESE CANDLE CHARTS

GREAT DEPRESSION

LAND

10 YEAR TREASURY NOTE

FANNIE MAE

GOLD

OIL FUTURES

BITCOIN

FOREX

DOGECOIN

NYSE — New York Stock Exchange
is the largest equities-based exchange in the world.
The purpose of the NYSE is to provide a central
marketplace for investors to buy and sell stock. —
enabling companies to list their shares and raise
capital from investors.

NASDAQ — was formed by the National Association of Securities Dealers (NASD) to function as a global electronic marketplace for buying and selling securities. NASDAQ enables investors to trade securities on a computerized system.

DJIA — the Dow Industrial Average is known as the **Dow Jones** and simply as the **Dow**. It is an index that measure the performance of **30** large companies listed on the NYSE and NASDAQ.

S&P 500 — the Standard & Poor's 500 (or the **S&P**) is an index that measures the performance of **500** large companies listed on exchanges in the United States.

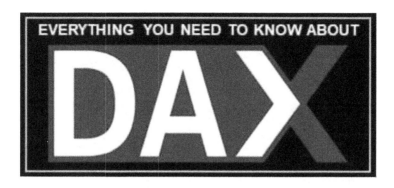

DAX — the DAX Performance Index — is a blue-chip index made up of **30** major German companies traded on the Frankfurt Stock Exchange.

STOCK MARKET — although most people think of Wall Street or the New York Stock Exchange — there are **stock markets**, **share markets**, or **equity markets** around the world which enable investors to buy and sell stocks which represent ownership interests in businesses.

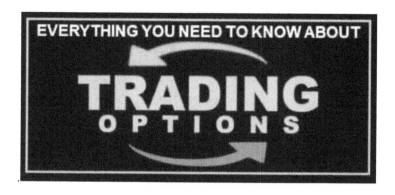

TRADING OPTIONS — trading options instead of the underlying instrument include offer these advantages:
- They may be less risky.
- They may be more cost efficient.
- They may provide higher returns.

An option is a contract that allows (but doesn't require) investors to buy the underlying security, ETF, or index at a predetermined price over a certain period of time. The price of an option is called a **premium**. Options do not represent ownership in any company.

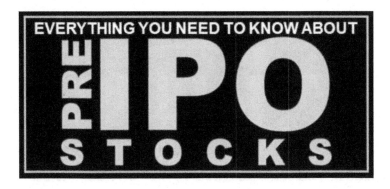

PRE IPO — Pre-**Initial Public Offering** Stocks. Although Pre-IPO Investing has a lot of sex appeal — it's not as simple or foolproof as it might sound. A Pre-IPO placement of stock is the sale of large block of stock before the shares are listed on a public stock exchange. Purchasers get the shares at a discount to the IPO price. **Do I have your attention yet?**

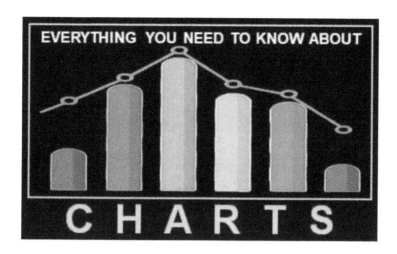

CHARTS are used for all types of investments to show prices plotted over a time frame and it shows the symbol of the security and exchange where it is traded —used for **technical analysis**.

JAPANESE CANDLE CHARTS were used by Japanese rice traders over 100 years ago — before Western traders even developed bar charts and point-and-figure charts. In the 1700's a Japanese rice trader noticed that rice market was influenced by the **emotions** of traders. Japanese Candle Charts visually display emotion through candlesticks of different colors to show the various size of price moves. Used for **technical analysis** to forecast short-term price moves.

THE GREAT DEPRESSION was ignited by the 1929 Stock Market Crash and lasted through the 1930. It was global in scope and was one America's darkest times.

LAND INVESTMENTS can be great, or they can be a waste of time and money of you don't know what you're doing — or don't have an advisor who does. Obviously, you want to purchase land cheap and hope that it will increase in value over time.

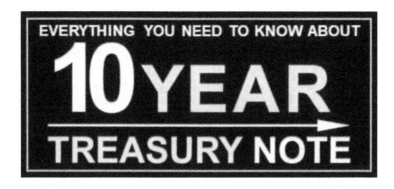

10 YEAR TREASURY NOTES are debt instruments issued by the United States Government paying interest at a fixed rate every six months and paying the face value of the note at maturity (10 years). Treasury yields always move in the opposite direction of treasury prices. The 10 Treasury note is the benchmark that guides other interest rates — including the 30 Year mortgage — it's important to watch.

FANNIE MAE — The Federal National Mortgage Association is an agency sponsored by the U.S. Government that is publicly traded under the ticker symbol **FNMA**. Fannie Mae's purpose is to expand **the secondary market** and make mortgage loans secure by packaging them into mortgage-backed securities **(MBS)**.

GOLD! Those four letters pretty much say it all! A Google search of those four letters returns about 25,270,000,000 results (1.14 seconds) — so what do you think about that? As an investment gold is the most popular of all the precious metals and there a lot of ways to invest in gold. Investors buy gold through futures contracts and options as a way of diversifying risk. Buy gold bullion or invest in gold jewelry, certificates, stocks, mutual funds, or ETFs — or you prospect for your own gold mine or pan for gold at Knott's Berry Farm.

BASICS OF
TRADING OIL FUTURES

Oil — also known as Black Gold and Texas Tea. Crude oil futures are contracts in which buyers and sellers of oil agree to deliver specific amounts of crude oil (barrels) on a given date in the future (that's why they're called **futures**). Investing in oil futures allows you to trade rising and falling oil prices. The two most popular types are Brent Crude and West Texas Intermediate. You can also invest in oil **options** giving you the right (but not the obligation) to buy or sell a specific amount of oil at a set price on a set future date.

BITCOIN. The founder of Bitcoin, Satoshi Nakamoto, is quoted as saying (in the early days of Bitcoin): "If you don't believe it or don't get it, I don't have the time to try to convince you, sorry." And that's *almost* everything you need to know about Bitcoin except that it's a **cryptocurrency** that's highly volatile because of its buy-sell cycle — and that it's highly controversial.

FOREX — Foreign Exchange Market is a global over the counter (decentralized) market for trading currencies. **Forex** determines the prices for every currency — and encompasses all aspects of foreign exchange trading: buying, selling, and exchanging currencies at current or determined prices. Trading Foreign Exchange — **FX** —involves a high degree of risk so *caveat emptor*. You can invest in foreign exchange in many ways, including: **Forex** (24-hour spot market where currencies are traded in pairs and traders are betting one currency will go up and the other one will go down); **Foreign Currency Futures**; **Foreign Currency Options**; **Exchange Traded Funds** (ETFs) and **Exchange Traded Notes** (ETNs); **Foreign Bold Funds**; and, **Foreign Currency Certificates of Deposit** (FCCDs).

DOGECOIN. Inspired by the Shiba Inu featured in the "Doge" meme — Dogecoin is a Lite-coin based cryptocurrency. It is still relatively cheap and may have the potential for great appreciation as a Crypto Heavy Hitter. Let's see!

EVERYTHING YOU NEED TO KNOW ABOUT

INVESTING

- You will never know everything you need to know about investing!
- Buy Low and Sell High OR
  Sell High and Buy Low.
- Pigs get slaughtered.
- Not all the Movers and Shakers on Wall Street make millions.
- You must QUICKLY learn how to cut your losses short.
- You don't need a Harvard Degree — or any degree — to be successful.
- The most successful investors are not in New York.
- Anyone can invest — but not everyone can become an *investor.*
- You don't need to start BIG to grow BIG — size doesn't matter.
- Wall Street trades and invests its own money MUCH differently than the traditional "buy and hold" strategies used by most of its clients — and so should YOU!
- At some point you will engage the services of a professional wealth manager and/or invest in hedge funds or private equity funds because you may realize that you don't have the time, inclination, or talent to manage and protect your own money.

224

HENRY PARK

ELEVEN

The older I get the more I see a straight path where I want to go. If you're going to hunt elephants, don't get off the trail for a rabbit.

— T. Boone Pickens

ELEVEN
OWNER'S MANUAL

Any product that needs a manual to work is broken.

— Elon Musk

Okay. Let's talk about all of the stuff you do not want to do on your Road to a Million.
- Do not pay commissions to a broker.
- Do not accept advice from a multi-level insurance salesperson posing as a "Financial Planner."
- Do not invest in mutual funds that charge a loan or high management fees
- Do not buy investment products from friends and family members.
- Do not try to manage your own portfolio unless you are a seasoned and accredited investor.
- Do not fall in love with a company or investment.
- Do not be afraid to take calculated risks.
- Do not trade on margin unless you can afford it.
- Do not believe everything people tell you — do your own research and due diligence.
-

227

Here are **seven steps** for you to take to jump start your trip:

1. **Have a vision.**
2. **Fugeddaboudit!**
3. **Do your homework.**
4. **Map out your trip.**
5. **Choose your vehicles.**
6. **Pick your travel mode.**
7. **Hit the road, Jack!**

Your trading success depends on your ability to understand these simple **7 Steps.** I suggest that you copy them in your own handwriting somewhere and memorize all of them. **Then take action.**

Taking these **7 Steps** as soon as possible will guarantee that you will be solidly on the way to create and protect great personal wealth. On the subject of **protection** — make sure that you seek the advice of a qualified, experienced, and appropriately licensed **Estate Planner** to review your **will, family trust,** and **tax strategy.** And, have a professional review your **life and accident insurance coverage.**

1

HAVE A VISION

So you have decided to take a trip to becoming a millionaire and are getting ready to jump onto your own **Road to a Million.** The first step, before you pack up and hit the road, is to have a vision of where you are going, when, and why. Create **your vision** below and review it daily (making any needed changes along the way). This is a paragraph long summary of what you created in **Chapter 7 — Your Road to a Million.**

2

FUGGEDABOUTIT!

You heard me right. Fuggeddaboudit! Forget about everything anybody who does not play a positive role in **your vision.** Forget about monsters, roadblocks, speedbumps, hazards, detours, and all of the other distractions that threaten to slow you down on your **Road to a Million.** Right now, make a list of what you need to fuggeddabout — and remember that it's a work in progress — so keep adding to your list along the way.

3

DO YOUR HOMEWORK

K nowledge is power. The more you learn — the more you'll earn. There is too much available information about wealth and investments — Google, Zooms, webinars, podcasts, blogs, radio and television shows, and yes, books. Don't allow information overload to paralyze you. You should have everything you need in this book to get started and everything you need to be successful by watching my weekly Zoom class. Just to make sure you don't miss anything along the way, jot down a few things you think you need to learn to become a millionaire.

4

MAP OUT YOUR TRIP

After you've done your homework you must map out your trip by inventorying your assets and liabilities and deciding where you want to go and when you want to get there. For example, you may write: "I want to start with $1,000 and grow it into $1,000,000 in three years." Then you'll chose the types of investments and management style that will get you to your destination on time.

5

CHOOSE YOUR VEHICLES

In Chapter Five we took a look at the various types of **investment vehicles** — from options to retirement accounts — and everything in between. Think of a sushi bar (my favorite food) and you will realize that there is a virtually unlimited offering of investment choices.

When most people think of sushi they think of "sushi rolls" —which is called Maki. Maki is rice and filling wrapped in seaweed. But there are other basic types of sushi — including: Nigiri, Sashimi, Uramaki, and Tamaki. When most people think of investments they think of stocks, bonds, mutual funds, and real estate. When you jump on your **Road to a Million** be ready, willing, and able to belly up to my investment sushi bar and try anything and everything that the I place in front of you. I will be your Itamae (sushi chef) — so get ready to have fun and eat a lot.

6

PICK YOUR TRAVEL MODE

Picking your travel mode may be challenging for you — kinda like the first time that you walk into a sushi bar and look at the colorful menu with all the new (and probably unfamiliar choices). So, let's look back at Chapter Six — Travel Options.

First on the menu is **DIY** – Drive It Yourself. This is a self-managed investment portfolio based on a "God knows where and what!" approach to getting rich. Maybe a little (or a lot) of Google searches, some (or a lot of) investment books, some "gurus" (Dave Ramsey and Susi Orman?) — and a little sage advice from the Motley Fools thrown in for good measure. Or **Mass Transit** — mutual funds or managed retirement accounts where you're along for the ride with everyone else. If you're a baller you may go **Charter** and have your own personal investment advisor. Finally, there's my personal **Party Bus.**

7

HIT THE ROAD, JACK!

Think about the last time you took a trip — a **road trip**. How far in advance did you plan for your trip? What did you do to get ready and how much time did you spend preparing for your trip?

Some of us plan trips for weeks if not months or even years. We explore possible destinations and compare routes. The most cautious of us take our vehicle in to have it serviced and safety checked — brakes, tires, windshield wipers...

And then there are those who just decide to hit the road. That's gonna be you this time. You're just going to grab a few things (clothes, sunscreen, iPhone) and climb aboard my **Party Bus**. I've got everything we need loaded and ready to roll — my bar is fully stocked, and we've got plenty of food — rave music is blasting, and navigation is set.

On the road again
Like a band of gypsies we go down the
    highway
We're the best of friends
Insisting the world keep turning our way
And our way
Is on the road again
Just can't wait to get on the road again

— Willie Nelson
On the Road Again (1979)

TWELVE

10

The Formula for the Rule of 72

$$\text{Years to Double} = \frac{72}{\text{Interest Rate}}$$

where:

Interest Rate = Rate of return on an investment

TWELVE
MILEAGE LOGS

It's not the years honey, it's the mileage.

— Harrison Ford

This section is for you to track your financial road trip from your initial investment of $1,000 to over $1,000,000 which requires you to double your money ten times. Help me with the math here.

Don't let the monsters in your mind fuck with you — they'll drive you crazy with all the "could haves" and "should haves".

Look back at the photo on the last page. I wasn't thinking "I could have had this Harley 30 years ago" or "I should have had this Harley 30 years ago". I was in the moment thinking **"Ride or die motherfuckers!"**

Building an investment portfolio is not like going on a diet or starting a fitness program where you have the majority of control on what you can do to control the outcome.

Managing and protecting a personal investment portfolio requires constant portfolio resizing and rebalancing.

You will have your own trade blotter but take the time to also record your "mileage" on the following pages for your **Road to a Million.**

0001000 — 0002000
Dollars

0002000 — 0004000
Dollars

(2)

0004000 — 0008000
Dollars

0008000 — 0016000
Dollars

0016000 — 0032000
Dollars

0032000 — 0064000
Dollars

0064000 — 0128000
Dollars

0128000 — 0256000
Dollars

0256000 — 0512000
Dollars

0512000 — 1024000
Dollars

$1,000,000 +

1000000 +
Dollars

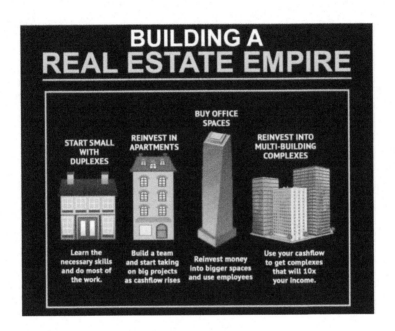

A long the way on **Your Road to a Million** it's important to remember that you have to rest and enjoy every nanosecond of your life. You need to ask yourself: "What's it all about Alfie?" For Spring Break this year Andrea and I escaped to Hawaii for a couple of weeks with our kids.

Henry Park

April 11 at 8:55 AM · 👥

...

By the time most of you wake up I will be on a plane ✈ on my way back home to the mainland. Usually for spring break i normally would travel abroad since it's one of the only times in the year where I can take 10 days off (including weekends) for spring break with the kids. This year because of Coronavirus I decided to come back to Hawaii. Hawaii is home to me. My brother was born here. I lived here till I was 5 years old. My dads side of the family all still lives here. I've been coming back and forth to these islands 🏝 since I was a kid. At least a 100 times. Anyone who has been here knows there's only so many things to do on the island. It's pretty small actually. You can drive around the whole island of Oahu in less than 4 hours. So coming back I was a little hesitant. What new things were there to see? Or do? I couldn't have been more wrong. I had no idea so many of my friends and family were here. Friends from high school. Andreas cousin. My kids friends from their school. We hung out with no less than 5 families while we were down here. It was fun to catch up. Good to relax and have good conversation. Disconnect from constantly talking about money and work. What I needed was a vacation!! And that's what Hawaii gave me. You know in Hawaii the "kamaaina" have a local saying. They say Aloha as a form of greeting, to say hello, welcome. But it's also a form of farewell, or to say goodbye. It's also used as an expression of love and affection. But more than just a word, aloha is also a way of life. And with that I say Aloha to all of you. Till next time

As an **investor** your mental state affects your performance and **trading** decisions. You need to invest quality time in rest and recreation — relax your mind. You cannot allow fatigue, depression, or negative emotions to distract you on **Your Road to a Million**. It's all about controlling your mind and emotions. I hope to see you soon in an online **Rest Area**.

C19 ECONOMICS

YOUR GUIDE TO PERSONAL AND BUSINESS FINANCE

ROBERT
MILLER

HENRY
PARK

LATINO
INVESTORS
ENTREPRENEURS
& ADVISORS

OFFICIAL 2021 GUIDE

ROBERT MILLER
HENRY PARK

FOREWORD BY
MR. ABC – AMADO HERNANDEZ

CONNECT WITH ME

 Henry@HenryParkNow.com

facebook.com/henry.park.940

 instagram.com/henryparkofficial

<u>My Facebook Group</u>
Henry Park's Road to a Million

My Weekly Zoom Classes
<u>Friday's — 5:00 PM (Pacific)</u>
Meeting I.D. 589 380 4727

You've made it to the end of **Henry Park's Road to a Million!** Congratulations. Maybe you have read the whole book or maybe you just skimmed through and have landed on this page. Anyway, here you are. You are on the page that really matters. This final page includes all the secret sauce — and all the magic. You have all the magic of increasing and protecting your personal wealth. These words are like Garth Brook's "third verse" of Friends in Low Places and Jimmy Buffet's "lost verse" in Margaritaville. The rest of the book has a specific structure and an intentional format. I made it easy to read with large fonts, a lot of air space, photos, and places for you to interact and make lots of notes. This page is much different. This is my final rant on what you need to do to become a millionaire (or billionaire). Smaller fonts and bigger words — no photos and no blank spaces. So here we go. First, forget everything you think you know about money and economics and order a copy of my book on Amazon — C19 Economics — so that you can read it as soon as you finish reading **Henry Park's Road to a Million.** I want you to understand that we are in a global political, social, and economic environment unlike any other time in history. It's critical that you "get it.". There are going to be more opportunities to get rich in the next ten years than you can even begin to imagine. But to get rich you need to believe that you can do it and you cannot let your own emotions get in your way. I have shared a lot of information in this book and have provided some tricks, secrets, and tools. But the bottom line is that **YOU** have to make it happen. Never lose sight of the fact that this is all about **Your Road to a Million** — it's not about Warren Buffet, Richard Branson, Mark Cuban, Elon Musk, or Jeff Bezos. It's not about Gordon Gekko or Jordan Belfort. And its not about Henry Park. We all have our stories. You know mine. I am a first-generation Korean American born in Guam (yes, that's part of the United States of America) who took a lot of shit growing up as a poor Asian kid in the Latino barrio. Now I don't have to take shit from anybody — and I don't. Why? Because I don't give a fuck about most of the shit that's going on around the world. I love my wife Andrea and our five children — Katie, Preston, Dylan, Audrey, and Dominic, more than life itself. And I am passionate about doing deals and making a significant impact on the world. That's why I wrote this book and host my Facebook Group and weekly Zoom Classes. So, what does this all mean to you? It means that, pure and simple, hope this book does more than "help" you because help can mean nothing. I want this book to turn your fucking world upside down. I want it to inspire you to change the way you look at the world, at the economy, at investments, about wealth, and — especially — how you look at yourself. I don't want you to read this book and think about it. I want you to take action right now and look in a mirror and scream at yourself and say: **"I am badass and I am going to become a fucking millionaire."** You don't need a coach or mentor or guru. You don't need a college degree or a lot of money to get started. But you must want it. You must want it like it's the "last fucking Coca Cola in the desert.

Did you figure out how to read the previous page? What did I say and what does it mean to you?

JOURNAL

_____

_____

_____

_____

_____

_____

_____

_____

_____

_____

_____

_____

_____

_____

_____

_____

_____

_____

_____

_____

_____

Date: _____

JOURNAL

Date: _____

JOURNAL

Date: _____

JOURNAL

Date: _____

JOURNAL

Date: _____

JOURNAL

Date: _____

JOURNAL

Date: _____

JOURNAL

Date: _____

JOURNAL

Date: _____

JOURNAL

Date: _____

JOURNAL

Date: _____

JOURNAL

Date: _____

IF SOMEONE OFFERS YOU AN AMAZING OPPORTUNITY BUT YOU ARE NOT SURE YOU CAN DO IT, SAY YES — THEN FIND OUT HOW TO DO IT LATER.

— Sir Richard Branson

Jean-Pierre Sarti: Before you leave I want to tell you something. Not about the others but about myself. I used to go to pieces. I'd see an accident like that and be so weak inside that I wanted to quit — stop the car and walk away. I could hardly make myself go past it. But I'm older now. When I see something really horrible, I put my foot down. Hard! Because I know that everyone else is lifting his.

Louise Frederickson: What a horrible way to win.

Jean-Pierre Sarti: No, there is no terrible way to win. There is only winning.

— *Grand Prix* (1966)

Made in the USA
Columbia, SC
12 September 2022